The feasts of Autolycus, the diary of a greedy woman

Elizabeth Robins Pennell

Nabu Public Domain Reprints:

You are holding a reproduction of an original work published before 1923 that is in the public domain in the United States of America, and possibly other countries. You may freely copy and distribute this work as no entity (individual or corporate) has a copyright on the body of the work. This book may contain prior copyright references, and library stamps (as most of these works were scanned from library copies). These have been scanned and retained as part of the historical artifact.

This book may have occasional imperfections such as missing or blurred pages, poor pictures, errant marks, etc. that were either part of the original artifact, or were introduced by the scanning process. We believe this work is culturally important, and despite the imperfections, have elected to bring it back into print as part of our continuing commitment to the preservation of printed works worldwide. We appreciate your understanding of the imperfections in the preservation process, and hope you enjoy this valuable book.

THE FEASTS OF AUTOLYCUS
THE DIARY OF A GREEDY WOMAN

EDITED BY ELIZABETH ROBINS PENNELL

AKRON, O.
THE SAALFIELD PUBLISHING COMPANY
CHICAGO   NEW YORK
1900

Copyright, 1896,
By The Merriam Company.

NOTE.—*These papers were first published in the "Pall Mall Gazette," under the heading, "Wares of Autolycus." It is due to the courteous permission of the editors of that Journal that they are now re-issued in book form.*

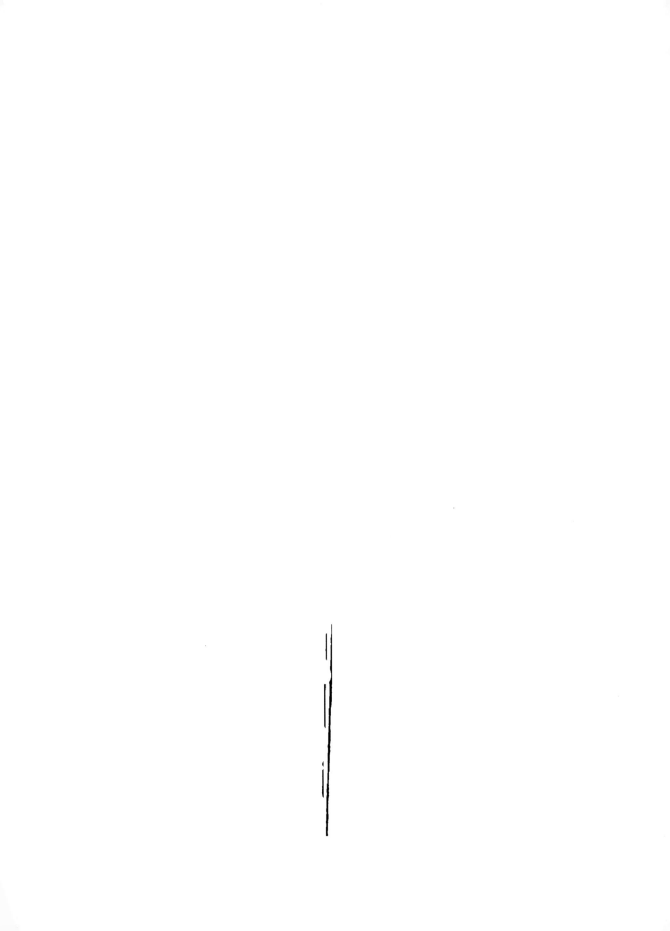

INTRODUCTION

I HAVE always wondered that woman could be so glib in claiming equality with man. In such trifling matters as politics and science and industry, I doubt if there be much to choose between the two sexes. But in the cultivation and practice of an art which concerns life more seriously, woman has hitherto proved an inferior creature.

For centuries the kitchen has been her appointed sphere of action. And yet, here, as in the studio and the study, she has allowed man to carry off the laurels. Vatel, Carême, Ude, Dumas, Gouffé, Etienne, these are some of the immortal cooks of history: the kitchen still waits its Sappho. Mrs Glasse, at first, might be thought a notable exception; but it is not so much the merit of her book as its extreme rarity in the first edition which has made it famous.

Woman, moreover, has eaten with as little

distinction as she has cooked. It seems almost —much as I deplore the admission—as if she were of coarser clay than man, lacking the more artistic instincts, the subtler, daintier emotions.

I think, therefore, the great interest of the following papers lies in the fact that they are written by a woman—a greedy woman. The collection, evidently, does not pretend to be a "Cook's Manual," or a "Housewife's Companion": already the diligent, in numbers, have catalogued *recipes*, with more or less exactness. It is rather a guide to the Beauty, the Poetry, that exists in the perfect dish, even as in the masterpiece of a Titian or a Swinburne. Surely hope need not be abandoned when there is found one woman who can eat, with understanding, the Feasts of Autolycus.

ELIZABETH ROBINS PENNELL.

CONTENTS.

	PAGE
THE VIRTUE OF GLUTTONY,	9
A PERFECT BREAKFAST,	17
TWO BREAKFASTS,	25
THE SUBTLE SANDWICH,	33
A PERFECT DINNER,	43
AN AUTUMN DINNER,	51
A MIDSUMMER DINNER,	59
TWO SUPPERS,	67
ON SOUP,	75
THE SIMPLE SOLE,	89
BOUILLABAISSE,	97
THE MOST EXCELLENT OYSTER,	105
THE PARTRIDGE,	117
THE ARCHANGELIC BIRD,	125
SPRING CHICKEN,	135
THE MAGNIFICENT MUSHROOM,	143
THE INCOMPARABLE ONION,	155
THE TRIUMPHANT TOMATO,	171

Contents.

	PAGE
A Dish of Sunshine,	179
On Salads,	191
The Salads of Spain,	205
The Stirring Savoury,	215
Indispensable Cheese,	223
A Study in Green and Red,	231
A Message from the South,	239
Enchanting Coffee,	249

THE VIRTUE OF GLUTTONY

GLUTTONY is ranked with the deadly sins; it should be honoured among the cardinal virtues. It was in the Dark Ages of asceticism that contempt for it was fostered. Selfish anchorites, vowed to dried dates and lentils, or browsing Nebuchadnezzar-like upon grass, thought by their lamentable example to rob the world of its chief blessing. Cheerfully, and without a scruple, they would have sacrificed beauty and pleasure to their own superstition. If the vineyard yielded wine and the orchard fruit, if cattle were sent to pasture, and the forest abounded in game, they believed it was that men might forswear the delights thus offered. And so food came into ill repute and foolish fasting was glorified, until a healthy appetite passed for a snare of the devil, and its gratification meant eternal damnation. Poor deluded humans, ever so keen to make the least of the short span of life allotted to them!

With time, all superstitions fail; and asceticism went the way of many another ingenious folly. But as a tradition, as a convention, somehow, it lingered longer among women. And the old Christian duty became a new feminine grace. And where the fanatic had fasted that his soul might prove comelier in the sight of God, silly matrons and maidens starved, or pretended to starve, themselves that their bodies might seem fairer in the eyes of man. And dire, indeed, has been their punishment. The legend was that swooning Angelina or tear-stained Amelia, who, in company, toyed tenderly with a chicken wing or unsubstantial wafer, later retired to the pantry to stuff herself with jam and pickles. And thus gradually, so it is asserted, the delicacy of women's palate was destroyed; food to her perverted stomach was but a mere necessity to stay the pangs of hunger, and the pleasure of eating she looked upon as a deep mystery, into which only man could be initiated.

In this there is much exaggeration, but still much truth. To-day women, as a rule, think all too little of the joys of eating. They hold lightly the treasures that should prove invaluable. They refuse to recognise that there is no less art in eating well than in painting well or writing well, and if their choice lay between swallowing a bun with a cup of tea in an aërated bread shop, and missing the latest picture show or doing without a new book, they would not hesitate; to the stodgy bun they would condemn themselves, though that way madness lies. Is it not true that the woman who would economise, first draws her purse-strings tight in the market and at the restaurant? With her milliner's bill she may find no fault, but in butcher's book, or grocer's, every halfpenny is to be disputed.

The loss is hers, but the generous-hearted can but regret it. Therefore let her be brought face to face with certain fundamental facts, and the scales will fall quickly from her eyes, and she will see the truth in all its splendour.

First, then, let her know that the love of good eating gives an object to life. She need not stray after false gods; she will not burden herself with silly fads, once she realizes that upon food she may concentrate thought and energy, and her higher nature—which to her means so much—be developed thereby. Why clamour for the suffrage, why labour for the redemption of brutal man, why wear, with noisy advertisement, ribbons white or blue, when three times a day there is a work of art, easily within her reach, to be created? All his life a Velasquez devoted to his pictures, a Shakespeare to his plays, a Wagner to his operas: why should not the woman of genius spend hers in designing exquisite dinners, inventing original breakfasts, and be respected for the nobility of her self-appointed task? For in the planning of the perfect meal there is art; and, after all, is not art the one real, the one important thing in life?

And the object she thus accepts will be her pleasure as well. For the *gourmande*, or glutton, duty and amusement go hand in hand. Her dainty devices and harmonies appeal to her imagination and fancy; they play gently with her emotions; they develop to the utmost her pretty sensuousness. Mind and body alike are satisfied. And so long as this pleasure endures it will never seem time to die. The ancient philosopher thought that time had come when life afforded more evil than good. The good of a pleasantly planned dinner outbalances the evil of daily trials and tribulations.

Here is another more intimate, personal reason which the woman of sense may not set aside with flippancy or indifference. By artistic gluttony, beauty is increased, if not actually created. Listen to the words of Brillat-Savarin, that suave and sympathetic *gourmet:* "It has been proved by a series of rigorously exact observations that by a succulent, delicate, and choice regimen, the external appearances of age are kept away for a long time. It gives more brilliancy to the eye, more freshness to the skin, more support to the muscles; and as it is certain in physiology that wrinkles, those formidable enemies of beauty, are caused by the depression of muscle, it is equally true that, other things being equal, those who understand eating are comparatively four years younger than those ignorant of that science." Surely he should have called it art, not science. But let that pass. Rejoice in the knowledge that gluttony is the best cosmetic.

And more than this: a woman not only grows beautiful when she eats well, but she is bewitchingly lovely in the very act of eating. Listen again, for certain texts cannot be heard too often: "There is no more pretty sight than a pretty *gourmande* under arms. Her napkin is nicely adjusted; one of her hands rests on the table, the other carries to her mouth little morsels artistically carved, or the wing of a partridge, which must be picked Her eyes sparkle, her lips are glossy, her talk cheerful, all her movements graceful, nor is there lacking some spice of the coquetry which accompanies all that women do. With so many advantages she is irresistible, and Cato, the censor himself, could not help yielding to the influence." And who shall say that woman, declaiming on the public platform, or "spanking" progressive principles into the child-man, makes a prettier picture?

Another plea, and one not to be scorned, is the new bond of union love of eating weaves between man and wife. "A wedded pair with this taste in common have once a day at least a pleasant opportunity of meeting." Sport has been pronounced a closer tie than religion, but what of food? What, indeed? Let men and women look to it that at table delicious sympathy makes them one, and marriage will cease to be a failure. If they agree upon their sauces and salads, what matter if they disagree upon mere questions of conduct and finance? Accept the gospel of good living and the sexual problem will be solved. She who first dares to write the great Food Novel will be a true champion of her sex. And yet women meet and dine together, and none has the courage to whisper the true secret of emancipation. Mostly fools! Alas! that it should have to be written!

And think—that is, if you know how to think —of the new joy added to friendship, the new charm to casual acquaintanceship, when food is given its due, and is recognised as something to be talked of. The old platitudes will fade and die. The maiden will cease to ask "What do you think of the Academy?" The earnest one will no longer look to Ibsen for heavy small talk. Pretence will be wiped away, conversational shams abolished, and the social millennium will have come. Eat with understanding, and interest in the dishes set before you must prove genuine and engrossing, as enthusiasm over the last new thing in art or ethics has never been—never can be. The sensation of the day will prove the latest arrangement in oysters, the newest device in vegetables. The ambitious will trust to her kitchen to win her reputation; the poet will offer lyrics and pastorals with every course; the painter will present in every dish a lovely scheme of colour.

Gross are they who see in eating and drinking nought but grossness. The woman who cannot live without a mission should now find the path clear before her. Let her learn first for herself the rapture that lies dormant in food; let her next spread abroad the joyful tidings Gluttony is a vice only when it leads to stupid, inartistic excess.

A PERFECT BREAKFAST

BREAKFAST means many things to many men. Ask the American, and he will give as definition: "Shad, beefsteak, hash, fried potatoes, omelet, coffee, buckwheat cakes, waffles, cornbread, and (if he be a Virginian) batter pudding, at 8 o'clock A.M. sharp." Ask the Englishman, and he will affirm stoutly: "Tea, a rasher of bacon, dry toast, and marmalade as the clock strikes nine, or the half after." And both, differing in detail as they may and do, are alike barbarians, understanding nothing of the first principles of gastronomy.

Seek out rather the Frenchman and his kinsmen of the Latin race. They know: and to their guidance the timid novice may trust herself without a fear. The blundering Teuton, however, would lead to perdition; for he, insensible to the charms of breakfast, does away with it altogether, and, as if still swayed by nursery rule, eats his dinner at noon—and may he long be left to enjoy it by himself! Therefore, in this, as in many other matters that cater to the higher pleasures, look to France for light and inspiration.

Upon rising—and why not let the hour vary according to mood and inclination?—forswear all but the *petit déjeuner:* the little breakfast of coffee and rolls and butter. But the coffee must be of the best, no chicory as you hope for salvation; the rolls must be crisp and light and fresh, as they always are in Paris and Vienna; the butter must be pure and sweet. And if you possess a fragment of self-respect, enjoy this *petit déjeuner* alone, in the solitude of your chamber. Upon the early family breakfast many and many a happy marriage has been wrecked; and so be warned in time.

At noon once more is man fit to meet his fellow-man and woman. Appetite has revived. The day is at its prime. By every law of nature and of art, this, of all others, is the hour that calls to breakfast.

When soft rains fall, and winds blow milder, and bushes in park or garden are sprouting and spring is at hand, grace your table with this same sweet promise of spring. Let rosy radish give the touch of colour to satisfy the eye, as chairs are drawn in close about the spotless cloth: the tiny, round radish, pulled in the early hours of the morning, still in its first virginal purity, tender, sweet, yet peppery, with all the piquancy of the young girl not quite a child, not yet a woman. In great bunches, it enlivens every stall at Covent Garden, and every greengrocer's window; on the breakfast-table it is the gayest poem that uncertain March can sing. Do not spoil it by adding other *hors d'œuvres;* nothing must be allowed to destroy its fragrance and its savour. Bread and butter, however, will serve as sympathetic background, and enhance rather than lessen its charm.

Vague poetic memories and aspirations stirred within you by the dainty radish, you will be in fitting humour for *œufs aux saucissons*, a dish, surely, invented by the Angels in Paradise. There is little earthly in its composition or flavour; irreverent it seems to describe it in poor halting words. But if language prove weak, intention is good, and should others learn to honour this priceless delicacy, then will much have been accomplished. Without more ado, therefore, go to Benoist's, and buy the little truffled French sausages which that temple of delight provides. Fry them, and fry half the number of fresh eggs. Next, one egg and two sausages place in one of those irresistible little French baking-dishes, dim green or golden brown in colour, and, smothering them in rich wine sauce, bake, and serve—one little dish for each guest. Above all, study well your sauce; if it fail, disaster is inevitable; if it succeed, place laurel leaves in your hair, for you will have conquered. "A woman who has mastered sauces sits on the apex of civilisation."

Without fear of anti-climax, pass suavely on from *œufs aux saucissons* to *rognons sautés*. In thin elegant slices your kidneys should be cut, before trusting them to the melted butter in the frying pan; for seasoning, add salt, pepper, and parsley; for thickening, flour; for strength, a tablespoonful or more of stock; for stimulus, as much good claret; then eat thereof and you will never repent.

Dainty steps these to prepare the way for the breakfast's most substantial course, which, to be in loving sympathy with all that has gone before, may consist of *côtelettes de mouton au naturel*. See that the cutlets be small and plump, well trimmed, and beaten gently, once on each side, with a chopper cooled in water. Dip them into melted butter, grill them, turning them but once that the juice may not be lost, and thank kind fate that has let you live to enjoy so delicious a morsel. *Pommes de terre sautées* may be deemed chaste enough to appear —and disappear—at the same happy moment.

With welcome promise of spring the feast may end as it began. Order a salad to follow: cool, quieting, encouraging. When in its perfection cabbage lettuce is to be had, none could be more submissive and responsive to the wooing of oil and vinegar. Never forget to rub the bowl with onion, now in its first youth, ardent but less fiery than in the days to come, strong but less imperious. No other garniture is needed. The tender green of the lettuce leaves will blend and harmonise with the anemones and tulips, in old blue china or dazzling crystal, that decorate the table's centre; and though grey may be the skies without, something of May's softness and June's radiance will fill the breakfast-room with the glamour of romance.

What cheese, you ask? Suisse, of course. Is not the month March? Has not the *menu*, so lovingly devised, sent the spring rioting through your veins? Suisse with sugar, and prolong the sweet dreaming while you may. What if work you cannot, after thus giving the reins to fancy and to appetite? At least you will have had your hour of happiness. Breakfast is not for those who toil that they may dine; their sad portion is the mid-day sandwich.

Wine should be light and not too many. The true epicure will want but one, and he may do worse than let his choice fall upon Graves, though good Graves, alas! is not to be had for the asking. Much too heavy is Burgundy for breakfast. If your soul yearns for red wine, be aristocratic in your preferences, and, like the Stuarts, drink Claret—a good St. Estéphe or St. Julien.

Coffee is indispensable, and what is true of coffee after dinner is true as well of coffee after breakfast. Have it of the best, or else not at all. For liqueur, one of the less fervent, more maidenly varieties, Maraschino, perhaps, or Prunelle, but make sure it is the Prunelle, in stone jugs, that comes from Chalon-sur-Saône. Bring out the cigarettes—not the Egyptian or Turkish, with suspicion of opium lurking in their fragrant recesses—but the cleaner, purer Virginian. Then smoke until, like the Gypsy in Lenau's ballad, all earthly trouble you have smoked away, and you master the mysteries of Nirvana.

TWO BREAKFASTS

Spring is the year's playtime. Who, while trees are growing green and flowers are budding, can toil with an easy conscience? Later, mere "use and wont" accustoms the most sensitive to sunshine and green leaves and fragrant blossoms. It is easy to work in the summer. But spring, like wine, goes to the head and gladdens the heart of man, so that he is fit for no other duty than the enjoyment of this new gladness. If he be human, and not a mere machine, he must and will choose it for the season of his holiday.

This is why in the spring the midday breakfast appeals with most charm. It may be eaten in peace, with no thought of immediate return to inconsiderate desk or tyrannical easel. A stroll in the park, a walk across the fields, or over the hills and far away, should be the most laborious labour to follow. It would be a crime, indeed, to eat a dainty breakfast, daintily designed and served, in the bustle and nervous hurry of a working day. But when the sunny hours bring only new pleasure and new capacity for it, what better than to break their sweet monotony with a light, joyous feast that worthily plays the herald to the evening's banquet?

It must be light, however: light as the sunshine that falls so softly on spotless white linen and flawless silver; gay and gracious as the golden daffodils in their tall glass. The table's ornaments should be few: would not the least touch of heaviness mar the effect of spring? Why, then, add to the daffodils? See, only, that they are fresh, just plucked from the cool green woodland, the morning dew still wet and shining on their golden petals, and make sure that the glass, though simple, is as shapely as Venice or Whitefriars can fashion it.

Daffodils will smile a welcome, if radishes come to give them greeting; radishes, round and rosy and crisp; there is a separate joy in the low sound of teeth crunching in their crispness. Vienna rolls (and London can now supply them) and rich yellow butter from Devon dairies carry out the scheme of the first gardenlike course.

Sweeter smiles fall from the daffodils, if now they prove motive to a fine symphony in gold; as they will if *omelette aux rognons* be chosen as second course. Do not trust the omelet to heavy-handed cook, who thinks it means a compromise between piecrust and pancake. It must be frothy, and strong in that quality of lightness which gives the keynote to the composition as a whole. Enclosed within its melting gold, at its very heart, as it were, lie the kidneys elegantly minced and seasoned with delicate care. It is a dish predestined for the midday breakfast, too beautiful to be wasted on the early, dull, morning hours; too immaterial for the evening's demands.

Its memory will linger pleasantly, even when *pilaff de volaille à l'Indienne* succeeds, offering a new and more stirring symphony in the same radiant gold. For golden is the rice, stained with curry, as it encircles the pretty, soft mound of chicken livers, brown and delicious. Here the breakfast reaches its one substantial point; but meat more heavy would seem vulgar and gross. The curry must not be too hot, but rather gentle and genial like the lovely May sunshine.

Now, a pause and a contrast. Gold fades into green. As are the stalks to the daffodils, so the dish of *petits pois aux laitues* to *pilaff* and *omelette*. The peas are so young that no device need be sought to disguise their age; later on, like faded beauty, they may have recourse to many a trick and a pose, but not as yet. The lettuce, as unsophisticated, will but emphasise their exquisite youth. It is a combination that has all the wonderful charm of infant leaves and tentative buds on one and the same branch of the spring-fired bush.

No sweet. Would not the artifice of jellies and cream pall after such a succession of Nature's dear tributes? Surely the *menu* should finish as it began, in entrancing simplicity. Port Salut is a cheese that smells of the dairy; that, for all its monastic origin, suggests the pink and white Hetty or Tess with sleeves well uprolled over curved, dimpling arms. Eat it with Bath Oliver biscuits, and sigh that the end should come so soon. Where the need to drag in the mummy at the close of the feast? The ancients were wise; with the last course does it not ever stare at you cruelly, with mocking reminder that eating, like love, hath an end?

Graves is the wine to drink with daffodil-crowned feast—golden Graves, light as the breakfast, gay as the sunshine, gladdening as the spring itself. Coffee completes the composition nobly, if it be black and strong And for liqueur, Benedictine, in colour and feeling alike, enters most fittingly into the harmony. Smoke cigarettes from Virginia, that southern land of luxuriant spring flowers.

There is no monotony in spring sunshine; why, then, let spring's breakfast always strike the same monotonous note? Another day, another mood, and so, as logical consequence, another *menu*. From your own garden gather a bunch of late tulips, scarlet and glowing, but cool in their shelter of long tapering leaves. Fill a bowl with them: it may be a rare bronze from Japan, or a fine piece of old Delft, or anything else, provided it be somewhat sumptuous as becomes the blossoms it holds. Open with that triumph of colour which would have enchanted a Titian or a Monticelli: the roseate salmon of the Rhine, smoked to a turn, and cut in thin slices, all but transparent. It kindles desire and lends new zest to appetite.

After so ardent a preparation, what better suited for ensuing course than *œufs brouillés aux pointes d'asperges?* the eggs golden and fleecy as the clouds in the sunset's glow; the asparagus points imparting that exqusite flavour which is so essentially their own. Cloudlike, the loveliness gradually and gracefully disappears, as in a poet's dream or a painter's impression, and spring acquires a new meaning, a new power to enchant.

Who, with a soul, could pass on to a roast or a big heating joint? More to the purpose is *ris de veau à la Toulouse*, the sweetbreads broiled with distinction, and then, in pretty fluted *caissons*, surrounded with *Béchamel* sauce and ravishing *ragoût* of mushrooms and cock's combs. They are light as a feather, but still a trifle flamboyant in honour of the tulips, while the name carries with it gaiety from the gay southern town of the *Jeux Floraux*.

Next, a salad is not out of place. Make it of tomatoes, scarlet and stirring, like some strange tropical blossoms decking the shrine of the sun. Just a suspicion of shallot in the bowl; the perfect dressing of vinegar and oil, pepper and salt; and the luxuriant tropics could not yield a richer and more fragrant offering. It is a salad that vies with Cleopatra in its defiance to custom. Love for it grows stronger with experience. The oftener it is enjoyed the greater the desire to enjoy it again.

Why, then, venture to destroy the impression it leaves with the cloying insipidity of some ill-timed sweet? It is almost too early for strawberries worth the eating, save in a *macédoine*, and they alone would come next in order, without introducing an element of confusion in the well-proportioned breakfast of spring. A savoury, too, would, at this special juncture, have its drawbacks. Cheese again best fulfils the conditions imposed. But now, something stronger, something more definite than Port Salut is called for; if Camembert prove the cheese of your choice, there will be no chance for criticism. One warning: see that it is ripe; for the Camembert that crumbles in its dryness is nothing short of iniquitous.

Tulips and tomatoes point to Claret as the wine to be drunk. Burgundy is for the evening, when candles are lighted, and the hours of dreaming have begun. St Estéphe, at noon, has infinite merit, and responds to the tulip's call with greater warmth than any white wine, whether from the vineyards of France or Germany, of Hungary or Italy. Coffee, as a matter of course, is to the elegantly-designed breakfast what the Butterfly is to the Nocturne. And when all is said, few liqueurs accord with it so graciously as Cognac; that is, if the dishes to precede it have tended to that joyful flamboyancy born of the artist's exuberance in moments of creation.

Eat either breakfast, or both; and be thankful that spring comes once a year.

THE SUBTLE SANDWICH

IF things yield themselves unto our mercy why should we not have the fruition of them, or apply them to our advantage? From evil, good may come; from the little, springs greatness. A reckless gamester, to defy the pangs of hunger, which might drag him from his beloved cards, brings to the gaming table slices of bread with ham between. If other men despise—or deplore, according to their passing mood—his folly, to their own pleasure and profit can they still turn his invention. The sandwich has become a universal possession for all time, though for a century the earl who created it has lain dead. His foibles should be forgotten, his one redeeming virtue remembered. For him a fair and spacious niche in the world's Valhalla.

A hero indeed is he who left the sandwich as an heirloom to humanity. It truly is the staff of life, a substantial meal for starving traveller or bread-winner; but none the less an incomparable work of art, a joy to the *gourmand* of fancy and discretion. The very name has come to be a pregnant symbol of holiday-making for all with souls to stir at the thought of food and drink. It is an inexhaustible stimulus to the imagination; to the memory a tender guide to the past's happiest days and hours.

For, in fancy, between the slices of bread, place thick, uncompromising pieces of beef or mutton, and to the Alps you are at once transported. Again, on the short, fragrant grass you sit; from its temporary snow-grave a little above, Perren or Imboden fetches the bottle of wine, ordinary enough in reality, nectar as you drink it there; Seiler's supplies you take from the faithful knapsack, opening paper package after paper package; and your feast of big, honest, no-nonsense-about-them sandwiches you devour with the appetite of a schoolboy, and the zeal of the convert to plain living and high mountain climbing.

Or, thin the slices, make them the covering for ham and tongue, or—if you be greatly favoured—for sardines and anchovies; and then memory will spread for you the banquet in the pleasant pastures that border the Cam, the willows bowering you from the August sun with shade, your boat moored to the cool bank; and with Claret cup, poured, mayhap, into old college tankards, you quench your thirst, while lazily you listen to the distant plashing of oars and lowing of kine, and all life drifts into an idle dream.

Or, the ham of Bayonne, the *pâté de foie gras* of Périgueux, you bury in the deep recesses of a long, narrow, crisp *petit pain*, and then, quick in a French railway carriage will you find yourself: a bottle of wine is at your side; the *Echo de Paris* lies spread on the seat before you; out of the window long lines of poplars go marching with you toward Paris, whither you are bound "to make the feast."

Grim and gruesome, it may be, are some of the memories evoked: ill-considered excursions to the bar of the English railway station, hasty lunches in chance bun shops, foolish testings of "ham and beef" limitations. But, henceforth, take heed to chasten your experience with the sandwich, that remembrance may not play you such scurvy tricks. Treat it aright with understanding and respect, and it will keep you in glad holiday humour, in the eating thereof as in the memory.

Life, alas! is not all play in Thames sunshine and keen Alpine air, or in hopeful journeying through the pleasant land of France. But in the everyday of stern work and doleful dissipation the sandwich is an ally of infallible trustworthiness and infinite resources. In the hour of need it is never found wanting. To dine well, authorities have proclaimed in *ex cathedrâ* utterance, you must lunch lightly; but not, therefore, does it follow that the light luncheon should be repellently prosaic. Let it be dainty—a graceful lyric—that it may fill you with hope of the coming dinner. And lyrical indeed is the savoury sandwich, well cut and garnished, served on rare faïence or old silver; a glass, or perhaps two, of Bordeaux of some famous vintage, to strengthen its subtle flavour.

An ally again at afternoon tea it proves, if at five o'clock drink tea you must; a mistake, surely, if you value your dinner. To belittle the excellence of crumpets and muffins well toasted, would be to betray a narrow mind and senseless prejudice; but these buttery, greasy delicacies in private should be eaten, where the ladies of Cranford sucked their oranges. And at the best their excellence is homely. In the sandwich well devised is something exotic and strange, some charm elusive and mysterious.

But let not the sandwich be of ham, except rarely, for the etherealized luncheon, the mystic tea. Reserve this well-meaning, but unpoetic, viand for the journey and the day of open-air sport, to which so admirably it is fitted. Nor so reserving it, will you be hampered in making what Dumas calls *tartines à l'Anglaise*. Infinity is at your disposal, if you be large and liberal enough to grasp the fact. One hundred numbered the varieties known to that genius of Glasgow, who, for his researches, has been honored by a place in dictionary and Encyclopædia. To these you may add, if time and leisure you find for a trip to Budapest and the famous Kügler's, where, with your tea, will be served such exquisite sandwiches, so original and many in their devices that you can but come away marvelling, in all eagerness to emulate the artist who designed them.

For the luncheon sandwich, choose from the countless treasures of the sea. Rapture is in the sardine, not the oiled from France, but the smoked from Norway; tunny fish or anchovies are dreams of delight; *caviar*, an ecstacy, the more delicious if a dash of lemon juice be added. And, if you would know these in perfection, use brown bread instead of white. Salmon is not to be scorned, nor turbot to be turned from in contempt; they become triumphs if you are not too niggardly with cayenne pepper; triumphs not unknown to Cheapside. Nor are the various so-called creams— of shrimps, of lobster, of salmon—altogether to be despised, and they, too, the better prove for the judicious touch of cayenne. But confine not your experiments to the conventional or the recommended. Overhaul the counter of the fishmonger. Set your wits to work. Cultivate your artistic instincts. Invent! Create! Many are the men who have painted pictures: few those who have composed a new and perfect sandwich.

Upon the egg, likewise, you may rely for inspiration—the humble hen's egg, or the lordly plover's. Hard-boiled, in thin slices (oh! the memories of Kügler's, and the Russian railway station, and the *hor d'œuvres*, Tartar-guarded sideboard, now awakened¹) or well grated; by itself, or in endless combinations, the egg will ever repay your confidence.

Upon sausage, also, you may count with loving faith. *Butterbrod mit Wurst—Wurst* and philosophy, these are the German masterpieces. And here, you may visit the *delicatessen* shop to good purpose. Goose-liver, Brunswick, garlic, Bologna, truffled—all fulfil their highest destiny, when in thinnest of thin slices, you lay them between slices no less thin of buttered bread—brown or white, as artistic appropriateness suggests—a faint suspicion of mustard to lend them piquancy.

Beef and mutton, when not cut in Alpine chunks, are comforting, and with mustard duly applied, grateful as well. Fowl and game, galantine and tongue, veal and brawn—no meat there is, whether fresh or boned or potted, that does not adapt itself gracefully to certain occasions, to certain needs. And here, again, be not slow to arrange new harmonies, to suggest new schemes. It should be your endeavor always to give style and individuality to your sandwiches.

Cheese in shavings, or grated, has great merit. Greater still has the cool cucumber, fragrant from its garden ground, the unrivalled tomato, the crisp, sharp mustard and cress. Scarce a green thing growing that will not lend itself to the true artist in sandwich-making. Lettuce, celery, water-cress, radishes—not one may you not test to your own higher happiness. And your art may be measured by your success in proving the onion to be the poetic soul of the sandwich, as of the salad bowl. For afternoon tea the dainty green sandwich is the daintiest of them all.

If to sweets your taste incline, then easily may you be gratified, though it be a taste smacking of the nursery and the schoolroom. Jams and marmalades you may press into service; chocolate or candied fruit. And sponge cake may take the place of bread, and, with strawberries between, you have the American strawberry short-cake.

But, whatever your sandwich, above all things see that its proportions be delicate and symmetrical; that it please the eye before ever the first fragment has passed into the mouth.

A PERFECT DINNER

FASHION and art have little in common. Save for chance, they would remain always as the poles apart. The laws of the one are transitory, of the other eternal; and as irreconcilable are they in the observance. Make then your choice between them, since no man may serve two masters.

Know that if ever the noble art of cookery be wrecked, it will be upon the quicksands of Fashion. In many ways is it threatened by the passing mode, but, above all others, one danger looms up before it, grim, relentless, tragic: the more awful because, to the thoughtless, at first it seems sweet as siren's singing. It is an evil born of the love of display and of the keen competition between Fashion's votaries. For they who would pose as delicate diners, think to eclipse their rivals by number of courses and bewildering variety. How to prolong the *menu*, rather than how to perfect it, is their constant study. In excess they would emulate the banquets of the ancients, though they are too refined by far to revive the old vomitories—the indispensable antidote. Dish follows dish, conceit is piled upon conceit; and with what result? Before dinner is half over, palates are jaded, "fine shades" can no more be appreciated, every new course awakens fear of the morrow's indigestion. Or else, pleasure is tempered by caution, a melancholy compromise; nothing is really eaten, the daintiest devices are but trifled with, and dinner is degraded into a torture fit for Tantalus. Surely, never was there a more cruel, fickle mistress than Fashion! Sad, immeasurably sad, the fate of her worshippers.

Art despises show, it disdains rivalry, and it knows not excess. A Velasquez or a Whistler never overloads his canvas for the sake of gorgeous detail. To the artist in words, superfluous ornament is the unpardonable sin. And so with the lovers of Gasterea, the tenth and fairest of the Muses. Better by far Omar Khayyam's jug of wine and loaf of bread, if both be good, than all the ill-regulated banquets of a Lucul-

A Perfect Dinner

lus. Who would hesitate between the feasts of Heliogabalus and the frugal fowl and the young kid, the raisins, figs, and nuts of Horace?

It matters not how many courses between oysters and coffee Fashion may decree, if, turning your back upon her and her silly pretensions, you devise a few that it will be a privilege for your guests to eat, a joy for them to remember. Bear in mind the master's model luncheon and its success. No *menu* could have been simpler; none more delicious. The table was laid for three, a goodly number, for all the slurs cast upon it. At each plate were "two dozen oysters with a bright golden lemon; at each end of the table stood a bottle of Sauterne, carefully wiped all except the cork, which showed unmistakably that it was long since the wine had been bottled." After the oysters roasted kidneys were served; next, truffled *foie-gras;* then the famous *fondue*, the beautiful arrangement of eggs beaten up with cheese, prepared over a chafing-dish at table, stimulating appetite by all the delights of anticipation. Fruit followed, and coffee; and last, two liqueurs, "one a spirit, to clear, and the other an oil, to soothe." Be not content to read, but go and do likewise!

Imagine a dinner planned on the same pattern, and the conventional banquet of the day soon will seem to you the monstrosity it is. Observe two all-important rules and you may not wander far wrong. One is to limit the number of courses; the other to serve first the substantial dishes, then those that are lighter, first the simpler wines, afterwards those of finer flavours.

The *hors d'œuvre*, however, is an exception. If too substantial it would defeat its end. It must whet the appetite, not blunt it. In its flavour must its strength lie; at once keen and subtle, it should stimulate, but never satisfy. An anchovy salad touches perfection; the anchovies—the boneless species from France—the olives skilfully stoned, the capers in carefully studied proportions, the yellow of the egg well grated, the parsley, chopped fine, must be arranged by an artist with a fine feeling for decorative effect, and the dressing of oil, vinegar, pepper, and salt, poured gently over the design so as not to destroy the poetry of line and colour. A crisp Vienna roll, with sweet fresh butter, makes an excellent accompaniment, but one to be enjoyed in moderation.

Crème Soubise is the soup to follow. Thick, creamy, onion-scented, the first spoonful enchants, and a glamour is at once cast over dinner and diners. Sufficing in itself, it needs neither Parmesan nor toast to enhance its merits. Like a beautiful woman, unadorned it is adorned the most.

Admirably, it prepares the way for oysters, deftly scalloped, with shallots and fragrant *bouquet garni* to lend them savour, and bread crumbs to form a rich golden-brown outer covering. If not unmindful of the eye's pleasure, you will make as many shells as there are guests serve the purpose of a single dish.

Without loitering or dallying with useless *entrées*, come at once to the one substantial course of the pleasant feast—and see that it be not too substantial. Avoid the heavy, clumsy, unimaginative joint. Decide rather for idyllic, *Tournedos aux Champignons;* the fillet tender and *saignant,* as the French say, the mushrooms, not of the little button variety, suggesting tins or bottles, but large and black and fresh from the market. Rapture is their inevitable sauce: rapture too deep for words. To share the same plate *pommes soufflées* may be found worthy.

None but the irreverent would seek to blur their impressions by eating other meats after so delectable a dish. Order, rather, a vegetable salad, fresh and soothing: potatoes, cauliflower, carrots, celery, a suspicion of garlic, and a sprinkling of parsley. Eat slowly; foolish is the impatient man who gallops through his pleasures in hot haste.

And now, be bold, defy convention, and do away with sweets. After so tender a poem, who could rejoice in the prose of pudding? But "a last course at dinner, wanting cheese, is like a pretty woman with only one eye." Therefore, unless you be blind to beauty, let cheese be served. Port Salut will do as well as another; neither too strong nor too mild, it has qualities not to be prized lightly.

Fruit is the sweet *envoy* to the Ballade of Dinner. And of all winter's fruits, the fragrant, spicy little Tangerine orange is most delicious and suggestive. Its perfume alone, to those who have dined discreetly, is a magic pass to the happy land of dreams. Conversation rallies, wit flashes, confidences are begotten over walnuts and almonds, and so, unless in surly, taciturn mood—as who could be after so exquisite a dinner?—let these have a place upon your *menu*.

See that your wines are as perfect of their kind as your courses. Too many would be a dire mistake. A good Sauterne, a light Burgundy will answer well if "of the first quality." Cheap, or of a poor vintage, they will ruin the choicest dish.

Upon coffee, too, much depends. It must be strong, it must be rich, it must be hot. But strength and richness may not be had unless it be fresh roasted and ground. Worse a hundredfold you may do than to mix Mocha with Mysore; theirs is one of the few happy unions. If romance have charm for you, then finish with a little glass of green Chartreuse—the yellow is for the feeble and the namby-pamby; powerful, indeed, is the spell it works, powerful and ecstatic.

And having thus well and wisely dined, the

cares of life will slip from you; its vexations and annoyances will dwindle into nothingness. Serene, at peace with yourself and all mankind, you may then claim as your right the true joys of living.

AN AUTUMN DINNER

Why sigh if summer be done, and already grey skies, like a pall, hang over fog-choked London town? The sun may shine, wild winds may blow, but every evening brings with it the happy dinner hour. With the autumn days foolish men play at being pessimists, and talk in platitudes of the cruel fall of the leaf and death of love. And what matter? May they not still eat and drink? May they not still know that most supreme of all joys, the perfect dish perfectly served? Small indeed is the evil of a broken heart compared to a coarsened palate or disordered digestion.

"Therefore have we cause to be merry!—and to cast away all care" Autumn has less to distract from the pleasure that never fails. The glare of foolish sunlight no longer lures to outdoor debauches, the soft breath of the south wind no longer breathes hope of happiness in Arcadian simplicity. We can sit in peace by our fireside, and dream dreams of a long succession of triumphant *menus*. The touch of frost in the air is as a spur to the artist's invention; it quickens ambition, and stirs to loftier aspiration. The summer languor is dissipated, and with the re-birth of activity is re-awakened desire for the delicious, the *piquante*, the fantastic.

Let an autumn dinner then be created! dainty, as all art must be, with that elegance and distinction and individuality without which the masterpiece is not Strike the personal note; forswear commonplace.

The glorious, unexpected overture shall be *soupe aux moules*. For this great advantage it can boast · it holds the attention not only in the short—all too short—moment of eating, but from early in the morning of the eventful day; nor does it allow itself to be forgotten as the eager hours race on. At eleven—and the heart leaps for delight as the clock strikes—the *pot-au-feu* is placed upon the fire; at four, tomatoes and onions—the onions white as the driven snow—communing in all good fellowship in a worthy saucepan follow; and at five, after an hour's boiling, they are strained through a sieve, peppered, salted, and seasoned. And now is the time for the mussels, swimming in a sauce made of a bottle of white wine, a *bouquet-garni*, carrot, excellent vinegar, and a glass of ordinary red wine, to be offered up in their turn, and some thirty minutes will suffice for the ceremony. At this critical point, bouillon, tomatoes, and mussels meet in a proper pot well rubbed with garlic, and an ardent quarter of an hour will consummate the union. As you eat, something of the ardour becomes yours, and in an ecstasy the dinner begins

Sad indeed would it prove were imagination exhausted with so promising a prelude. Each succeeding course must lead to new ecstasy, else will the dinner turn out the worst of failures. In *turbot au gratin*, the ecstatic possibilities are by no means limited. In a chaste silver dish, make a pretty wall of potatoes, which have been beaten to flour, enlivened with pepper and salt, enriched with butter and cream—cream thick and fresh and altogether adorable—seasoned with Parmesan cheese, and left on the stove for ten minutes, neither more nor less; let the wall enclose layers of turbot, already cooked and in pieces, of melted butter and of cream, with a fair covering of bread-crumbs, and rely upon a quick oven to complete the masterpiece.

After so pretty a conceit, where would be the poetry in heavy joints or solid meats? *Ris de veau aux truffes* surely would be more in sympathy; the sweetbreads baked and browned very tenderly, the sauce fashioned of truffles duly sliced, marsala, lemon juice, salt and *paprika*, with a fair foundation of benevolent bouillon. And with so exquisite a dish no disturbing vegetable should be served.

And after? If you still hanker for the roast beef and horseradish of Old England, then go and gorge yourself at the first convenient restaurant. Would you interrupt a symphony that the orchestra might play "God save the Queen"? Would you set the chorus in "Atalanta in Calydon" to singing odes by Mr. Alfred Austen? There is a place for all things, and the place for roast beef is not on the ecstatic *menu*. Grouse, rather, would meet the diner's mood— grouse with memories of the broad moor and purple heather. Roast them at a clear fire, basting them with maternal care. Remember that they, as well as pheasants and partridges, should " have gravy in the dish and bread-sauce in a cup." Their true affinity is less the vegetable, however artistically prepared, than the salad, serenely simple, that discord may not be risked. Not this the time for the bewildering *macédoine*, or the brilliant tomato. Choose, instead, lettuce; crisp cool *Romaine* by choice. Sober restraint should dignify the dressing; a suspicion of chives may be allowed; a sprinkling of well-chopped tarragon leaves is indispensable. Words are weak to express, but the true poet strong to feel the loveliness now fast reaching its climax.

It is autumn, the mood is fantastic: a sweet, if it tend not to the vulgarity of heavy puddings and stodgy pies, will introduce an amusing, a sprightly element *Omelette soufflée* claims the privilege. But it must be light as air, all but ethereal in substance, a mere nothing to melt in the mouth like a beautiful dream. And yet in melting it must yield a flavour as soft as the fragrance of flowers, and as evanescent. The sensation must be but a passing one that piques the curiosity and soothes the excited palate. A dash of orange-flower water, redolent of the graceful days that are no more, another of wine from Andalusian vineyards, and the sensation may be secured.

By the law of contrasts the vague must give way to the decided. The stirring, glorious climax after the brief, gentle interlude, will be had in *canapé des olives farcies*, the olives stuffed with anchovies and capers, deluged with cayenne, prone on their beds of toast and girded about with astonished watercress.

Fruit will seem a graceful afterthought; pears all golden, save where the sun, a passionate lover, with his kisses set them to blushing a rosy red; grapes, purple and white and voluptuous; figs, overflowing with the exotic sweetness of their far southern home; peaches, tender and juicy and desirable. To eat is to eschew all prose, to spread the wings of the soul in glad poetic flight. What matter, indeed, if the curtains shut out stormy night or monstrous fog?

Rejoice that no blue ribbon dangles unnecessarily and ignominiously at your buttonhole. Wine, rich wine to sing in the glass with "odorous music," the autumn dinner demands. Burgundy, rich red Burgundy, it should be; Beaune or Pomard as you will, to fire the blood and set the fancy free. And let none other but yourself warm it; study its temperature as the lover might study the frowns and smiles of his beloved. And the "Spirit of Wine" will sing in your hearts that you too may triumph

> In the savour and scent of his music,
> His magnetic and mastering song.

And the Burgundy will make superfluous Port and Tokay, and all the dessert wines, sweet or dry, which unsympathetic diners range before them upon the coming of the fruit.

Drink nothing else until wineglass be pushed aside for cup of coffee, black and sweet of savour, a blend of Mocha and Mysore. Rich, thick, luxurious, Turkish coffee would be a most fitting epilogue. But then, see that you refuse the more frivolous, feminine liqueurs. Cognac, old and strong-hearted, alone would meet the hour's emotions—Cognac, the gift of the gods, the immortal liquid. Lean back and smoke in silence, unless speech, exchanged with the one kind spirit, may be golden and perfect as the dinner.

A MIDSUMMER DINNER

AT midsummer, the *gourmand* subsists chiefly on hope of the good time coming. The 12th ushers in season of glorious plenty. But, for the moment, there is a lull in the market's activity. Green things there are in abundance; but upon green things alone it is not good for man to live. Consult the oracle; turn to the immortal, infallible "Almanack," and confirmation of this sad truth will stare you in the face plainly, relentlessly. Sucking-pig is sole consolation offered by benevolent De la Reynière to well-nigh inconsolable man. But what a poem in the sucking-pig that gambols gaily over his pages: a delicious roasted creature, its little belly stuffed full of liver and truffles and mushrooms, capers, anchovies, aromatic pepper, and salt, all wrought together into one elegant *farce;* while in dish apart, as indispensable acolyte, an orange sauce waits to complete the masterpiece! *En daube,* this amiable little beast is not to be despised, nor *en ragoût* need it be dismissed with disdain, though, let man of letters beware! The Society of Authors, with his welfare at heart, should warn him while still there is time. What zest might be given to the savourless *Author*, their organ, were its columns well filled with stately and brilliant discourses upon food and good eating. How the writer of delicate perceptions should eat: is that not, as subject, prettier and more profitable far than how much money he can make by publishing here and lecturing there?

The poor *gourmand*, in sorry plight during midsummer's famine, may seek blessed light also from Filippini, Delmonico's cook. Out of the fulness of his heart he speaketh, leaving not one of August's thirty-one shortening days without elaborate *menu*. But London must fast while New York feasts. At Delmonico's, happy diners may smile gracious welcome to Lima beans and sweet corn, to succotash and eggplant, to chicken *à l'okra* and clam chowder, but what hope for the patrons of Verrey's and Nichol's? What hope, unless, forthwith, they emigrate to that promised land beyond the broad Atlantic? For the rest, Filippini reveals not the originality, the invention that one would have hoped from him, even at the season when men are struck dead by the sun in the streets of his dear town of adoption. Roast turkey, with cranberry sauce, is suggestive of November's drear days; Brussels sprouts sum up greengrocers' resources in midwinter. But why falter? Hope need never be abandoned by the wise, whose faith is strong in himself.

The season presents difficulties, but the beautiful dinner may still be designed. To meet August's flaming mood, it should be rich, and frankly voluptuous. Let flowers that bespeak autumn's approach and the fulness of harvest give the dinner its keynote. In Delft bowl, of appropriate coarseness, heap the late summer's first dahlias, all scarlet and gold as London's sunset at the fall of the year. To the earth's ripeness and fertility their bold, unabashed hues bear loud and triumphant witness.

Let the soup be at once tribute and farewell to spring that has gone. Regret will be luxuriously expressed in *purée de petits pois*; spinach added to the fresh peas to lend flavour and colour, a dash of sugar for sweetness' sake, a pinch of *paprika* to counteract it, a suspicion of onion to strengthen it. Arrowroot, in discreet measure, will answer for thickening, and impart more becoming consistency even than flour. Pleasure in the eating will be tempered by sorrow in the prospect of parting, and therefore intensified a hundredfold. Where the joy in possession but for the ever-present fear of loss?

With the second course, banish regret. Forget yesterday; be indifferent to to-morrow; revel riotously in to-day. *Hure de saumon à la Cambacérès* will point out the way to supreme surrender. Close to the head, the delicate silver-rose of the fish must be cut in lavish proportions; braised gently, its removal to the dish that is waiting is signal to surround it with truffles and mushrooms and stoned olives —garland beyond compare; a sauce of drawn butter, seasoned with *paprika* and lemon juice and parsley, is essential accompaniment. And now the present truly has conquered!

The third course must not betray the second's promise. Gay and fantastic, it must be well able to stand the dread test of comparison.

Rognons d'agneau à l'épicurienne enters nobly into the breach; the lamb's dainty kidneys are split and grilled with decorum, their fragrant centres are adorned with sympathetic *sauce Tartare*, golden potatoes *à la Parisienne* insist upon serving as garniture, and Mr. Senn demands, as finishing touch, the stimulating seduction of *sauce Poivrade*. Who now will say that August is barren of delicious devices?

To follow: *poulet sauté à l'Hongroise*, the clash of the Czardas captured and imprisoned in a stew-pan. With the Racoczy's wild drumming stirring memory into frenzy, stew the fowl, already cut into six willing pieces, with butter, a well-minced onion, pepper—*paprika* by choice—and salt; ten minutes will suffice—how, indeed, endure the strain a second longer? Then to the notes of the cymbal, moisten with *Béchamel* sauce and fair quantity of cream, and rejoice in the fine Romany rapture for just twenty minutes more. Decorate with *croûtons*, and send fancy, without fetters, wandering across the plains and over the mountains of song-bound Magyarland. To play the gypsy, free as the deer in the forest, as the bird in the air, is not this as it should be in the month, more than all others, pledged to *pleinairisme?* Insipid, as life without love, is the dinner without imagination.

Vegetables have no special place in the scheme of August's dinner. But a salad will not come amiss. Remember, the feast is ordered in sheer voluptuousness of spirit. The fifth course calls for the scarlet splendour of tomatoes; and the presiding dahlias, in bowl of Delft, clamour for the gold of *mayonnaise* sauce to carry out the exulting trumpeting harmony. A hint, here, to the earnest, ambitious *gourmand;* if cream be worked, deftly and slowly, into the thickening sauce, sublime will be the results.

A sweet, at this juncture, would err if overchaste in conception. Picture to yourself the absurd figure cut by tapioca pudding or apple dumpling on conscientiously voluptuous *menu?* A *macédoine méringuée* would have more legitimate claim to close the banquet with distinction. August supplies fruit without stint: plums and greengages and apricots and nectarines and peaches and pears and grapes and bananas; all join together to sweet purpose, with ecstatic intent; a large wine-glass of Claret, a generous sprinkling of Cognac will guard against puerility. The protecting *méringue* should be crisp and pale golden brown; and later it will need the reinforcement of thick luscious cream.

A sweet fails to delight, unless a savoury comes speedily after. *Caviar de Russie en crêpes* is worthy successor of *macédoine méringuée*. Mingle cream with the *caviar*, and none who eats will have cause to complain. It reconciles to the barbarous, even where Tolstoi and Marie Bashkirtseff may have failed.

To dally with fruit is graceful excuse to linger longer over wine. Plums and greengages, their bloom still fresh, their plump roundness never yet submitted to trial by fire, figs—pale northern ghosts, alas!—peaches, grapes, make exquisite interlude—between dinner and coffee. Refrain not: abstinence, of all follies created by man, is the most wicked, the most unpardonable.

Drink Chambertin, that the song in your heart may be fervent and firm. Drink, that your courage may be strong for the feasting. Shake off the shackles of timidity Be fearless and brave, turning a deaf ear to the temptations of the temperate. To be moderate at midsummer is to disregard the imperative commands of immoderate nature.

Coffee, made as the Turks make it, will bring languorous, irresistible message from the sensuous East. *Fine Champagne* will add the energy of the fiery West. Adorable combination! Oh, East is East, and West is West; but the twain the day of the August dinner shall meet.

TWO SUPPERS

TRADITION is a kindly tyrant. Why then strive to shake off its shackles? To bow the neck gladly beneath the yoke is at times to win rich reward, first in charm of association, and then in pleasantness of actual fact.

Is there not a tradition in England that supper is more appropriate to the quiet of Sunday evenings than dinner? No use to ask whence it arose or whither it leads. There it is, though many would evade it as senseless makeshrift. To forswear dinner for all time and eternity would be worse than folly; it is life's most solemn, most joyous ceremony. But once and again, for dear sake of contrast, to find a seducing substitute is wisdom in a world where all pleasures fail, and man is constant to one thing never. And now that summer has come and holds the green earth in its ardent embrace, now that days are long, and sweetest hours are those when the sun sinks low, there is new delight in the evening meal that leaves one free to dream in the twilight, that does not summon one indoors just as all outdoors is loveliest. Supper on every day in the week would be a mistake; but on one in seven it may well be commended, especially when the month is June. In the afternoon, tea is served in the garden, or whatever London can offer in the garden's stead. There are a few strawberries in a pretty old porcelain dish to lend an air of dainty substance, and there is rich cream in which they may hide their pretty blushes; and there is gay talk and happy silence. Indolent hours follow. Is it not Sunday, and are not all weekly cares pigeon-holed out of sight?

Nor do the advantages of the occasional supper end here. It is excellent excuse for the ice-cold banquet which in the warm summertime has its own immeasurable virtues. A supper should be cold; else it deteriorates into mere sham dinner Never do cold dishes seem more delicious than when cruel thermometer is at fever heat. You see? There is logic in the Sunday evening supper, at this season of all seasons for love, and eating, and drinking.

But supper does not mean, necessarily, veal and ham pie, above which British imagination dares not soar. It is not limited to the half-demolished joint—sad wreck of midday's meal. It may be as fair and harmonious as dinner itself, as noble a tribute to the artist, as superb a creation. Only the thoughtless and prosaic will dismiss it carelessly in the ordering, believing that any odds and ends will answer. Whatever is left over is to many the one possible conception of the late evening meal. But the *gourmand*, exulting in his gluttony, makes of it a work of art, good in the eating, good in the remembrance thereof.

Summer allows wide scope for his fertile fancy. He may begin with salmon, refreshing to the eye in its arrangement of pale silver and rose, cold as the glaciers of Greenland after its long hours of repose on voluptuous bed of ice. A *mayonnaise* sauce, creamy and rich, turning the silver to gold, like a fairy godmother of legend, is the cherished accompaniment. The feeling of wonder, aroused in the hours of watching under the trees, being still uppermost, it will seem as if the soft hues of the afterglow had been embodied in this exquisite prologue, with its rose and citron, its gold and soft grey tints.

Tender spring chickens may then give greeting to the summer-time. They also will have spent hours in close communion with solid blocks of ice, and will be as cool as the breezes that blow over the high snow fields of Switzerland. For, be it noted in passing, without a refrigerator the perfect supper is sheer impossibility. Success depends largely upon temperature. Lukewarm supper would be as detestable as a lukewarm dinner. With the innocent chickens, chilling and chaste, a green salad will be as appropriate as edelweiss on Alpine slopes. It should be made of the hearts of the youngest of young cabbage lettuces, touched with onions, and fatigued with the one most admirable salad dressing that man ever devised. Linger as long as may be, for this surely is one of the beautiful moments that repay the artist for his toiling and his intervals of despair.

Asparagus will prove most seemly successor. Let it also be cold beyond suspicion. A sauce of vinegar and oil, pepper and salt, force it to yield its most subtle sweetness. It will prove another course to call for lingering. Unless happiness be realised, of what use is it to be happy? He who is not conscious of pleasure when he eats is not worthy to sit at table with the elect. Like the animals, he is content to feed, and the art of the cook is, alas! lost upon him.

A savoury at this banquet would be superfluous. The presence of cheese would be but deference to convention, and faithfulness to tradition does not demand as its price sacrifice of all freedom in detail. The asparagus would be dishonoured were it to give place to aught more substantial than strawberries. Sometimes in the day's *menu*, as in a decorative scheme, loveliness is enhanced by repetition. As a second curve emphasises the grace of the first, so strawberries at supper carry out with great elegance the strawberry scheme of afternoon tea. Pretty hillocks of sugar, and deep pools of cream, make a rich setting for this jewel among fruits.

The wine, clearly, should be white, and it,

too, should be iced—remember the month is June. Few Rhine wines could consistently refuse to be pressed into service. But French vineyards have greater charm than German, though the Lorelei may sing in near waters, and to Graves, or Barsac, preference will be wisely proffered.

Be fearful of striking a false note. See that the coffee, black and strong though it be, is as cold as wine and salmon, chicken and salad. And pour the green Chartreuse into glasses that have been first filled with crushed ice. And as you smoke your cigarette, ask yourself if the Sunday evening supper tradition be not one crying for preservation at all costs.

When another week has rolled by and disappeared into the *Ewigkeit*, vary the *menu*. An element of the *bizarre*, the strange, the unaccustomed, often lends irresistible piquancy. Be faithful to the refrigerator, however fickle to other loves. Open the banquet with a stirring salad fashioned of red herring and potatoes, and, perhaps, a few leaves of lettuce. It savours of the sensational, and stimulates appetite.

That disappointment may not ensue, desert well-trodden paths, and, borrowing from Germany, serve a dish of meat, amusing in its quaint variety. Slices of lamb may provide a pretty centre, surrounding them, scatter slices of the sausage of Brunswick and Bologna, here and there set in relief against a piece of grey *Leberwurst*. As garniture, encircle the dish with a garland of anchovies, curled up into enchanting little balls, and gherkins, and hard-boiled eggs cut in delicate rounds. Memories will crowd fast upon you as you eat; memories of the little German towns and their forgotten hilltops, visited in summers long since gone, of the little German inn, and the friendly landlord, eager to please; of the foaming mugs of beer, and the tall, slender goblets of white wine. Before supper is done, you will have travelled leagues upon leagues into the playtime of the past.

Cheese now is as essential as it would have been intrusive in the other *menu*. Gruyère should be your choice, and if you would have it of fine flavour, seek it not at the English cheesemonger's, but at the little German *delica-*

tessen shop. Brown bread would best enter into the spirit of the feast.

As epilogue, fruit can never be discordant, and what fruit in early June insists upon being eaten with such sweet persistency as the strawberry. But, on your German evening, fatigue it with Kirsch, leave it on its icy couch until the very last minute, and memories of the Lapérouse will mingle with those of the smoky inn of the Fatherland.

Is there any question that Hock is the wine, when sausage and red herring and Gruyère cheese figure so prominently in the *menu's* composition? Drink it from tall slender glass, that it may take you fully into its confidence. Coffee need not be iced. In fact, it should positively be hot—can you doubt it? And Cognac now will prove more responsive to your mood than Chartreuse. There is no written law to regulate these matters. But the true artist needs no code to guide him. He knows instinctively what is right and what is wrong, and doubts can never assail him.

ON SOUP

"When all around the wind doth blow," draw close the curtains, build up a roaring fire, light lamp and candles, and begin your dinner with a good—*good*, mind you—dish of soup. Words of wisdom are these, to be pondered over by the woman who would make her evening dinner a joyful anticipation, a cherished memory.

Soup, with so much else good and great, is misunderstood in an England merrier than dainty in her feasting. Better is this matter ordered across the Border. For the healthy-minded, Scotch mists have their compensation in Scotch broth; odoriferous and appetising is its very name. But in England, soup long since became synonymous with turtle, and the guzzling alderman of legend. Richness is held its one essential quality—richness, not strength. Too often, a thick, greasy mess, that could appeal but to the coarsest hunger, will be set before you, instead of the dish that can be comforting and sustaining both, and yet meddles not with the appetite. It should be but a prelude to the meal—the prologue, as it were, to the play—its excellence, a welcome forecast of delights to follow, a welcome stimulus to light talk and lighter laughter. Over *Julienne* or *bisque* frowns are smoothed away, and guests who sat down to table in monosyllabic gloom will plunge boldly into epigrammatic or anecdotic gaiety ere ever the fish be served.

Magical, indeed, is the spell good soup can cast Of its services as medicine or tonic, why speak? Beef tea gives courage to battle with pain and suffering; *consommé* cheers the hours of convalescence. Let all honour be done to it for its virtues in the sick-room; but with so cheerful a subject, it is pleasanter to dwell on its more cheerful aspects.

More legitimate is it to consider the happy part it plays in the traveller's programme. And for this—it must be repeated, as for all the best things in the *gourmand's* life—one journeys to France. But first remember—that contrast may add piquancy to the French *menu*—the fare that awaits the weary, disconsolate traveller at English railway station: the stodgy bun, Bath and penny varieties both, and the triangular sandwich ; the tea drawn overnight, and the lukewarm bovril, hopelessly inadequate substitute for soup freshly made from beef or stock. At a luncheon bar thus wickedly equipped, eating becomes what it never should be!—a sad, terrible necessity, a pleasureless safeguard against pangs of hunger, a mere animal function, and therefore a degradation to the human being educated to look upon food and drink—even so might the painter regard his colours, the sculptor his clay and marble—as means only to a perfect artistic end.

Or, consider also, to make the contrast stronger, the choicest banquet American railways, for all the famed American enterprise, provide. To journey by the "Pullman vestibuled train" from New York to Chicago is luxury, if you will. Upon your point of view depends the exact amount of enjoyment yielded by meals eaten while you dash through the world at the rate of eighty miles an hour, more or less, and generally less. There is charm in the coloured waiters, each with gay flower in his button-hole, and gayer smile on his jolly, black face; there is pretence in the cheap, heavy, clumsy Limoges off which you eat, out of which you drink, in the sham silver case in which your Champagne bottle is brought, if for Champagne you are foolish enough to call. But bitterness is in your wine cup, for the wine is flat; heaviness is in your breakfast or dinner, for bread is underdone and sodden, and butter is bad, and the endless array of little plates discourages with its suggestion of vulgar plenty and artless selection; and all is vanity and vexation, save the corn bread—the beautiful golden corn bread, which deserves a chapter to itself— and the fruit: the bananas and grapes, and peaches and oranges, luscious and ravishing as they seldom are on any but American soil. Nor will you mend matters by bestowing your patronage upon the railway restaurants of the big towns where you stop: the dirty, fly-bitten lunch counters. Pretentious, gorgeous, magnificent, they maybe; but good, no! All, even the privilege of journeying at the rate of eighty miles an hour, would you give for one bowl of good soup at the Amiens *buffet*.

For, when everything is said, it is the soup which makes travelling so easy and luxurious in France. A breakfast, or a dinner, of courses, well-cooked, and well-served into the bargain, you may eat at many a wayside station. Wine, ordinary as its name, perhaps, but still good and honest, is to be had for a paltry sum whenever the train may stop. Crisp rolls, light *brioches* tempt you to unwise excesses. Not a province, scarce a town, but has its own special dainty; nougat at Montélimart, sausages at Arles, *pâté de foie gras* at Pèrigueux; and so you might go on mapping out the country according to, not its departments, but its dishes. These, however, the experienced traveller would gladly sacrifice for the delicate, strong, refreshing, inspiriting *bouillon*, served at every *buffet*. This it is which helps one to forget fatigue and dust and cinders, and the odious Frenchman who will have all the windows shut. *Bouillon*, and not wine, gives one new heart to face the long night and the longer miles. With it the day's journey is well begun and well ended. It sustains and nourishes; and, better still, it has its own æsthetic value; perfect in itself, it is the one perfect dish for the place and purpose. No wonder, then, that it has kindled even Mr. Henry James into at least a show of enthusiasm; his bowls of *bouillon* ever remain in the reader's memory, the most prominent pleasures of his "Little Tour in France."

Equally desirable in illness and in health, during one's journeys abroad and one's days at home, why is it then that soup has never yet been praised and glorified as it should? How is it that its greatness has inspired neither ode nor epic; that it has been left to a parody— clever, to be sure, but cleverness alone is not tribute sufficient—in a child's book to sing its perfections. It should be extolled, and it has been vilified; insults have been heaped upon it; ingratitude from man has been its portion. The soup tureen is as poetic as the loving cup; why should it suggest but the baldest prose to its most ardent worshippers?

"Thick or clear?" whispers the restaurant waiter in your ear, as he points to the soups on the bill of fare. "Thick or clear,"—there you have the two all-important divisions. In that simple phrase is expressed the whole science of soupmaking; face to face with first principles it brings you. But whether you elect for the one or the other, this great fundamental truth there is, ever to be borne in mind: let fresh meat be the basis of your *consommé* as of your *bisque*, of your *gumbo* as of your *pâtes d'Italie*. True, in an emergency, Liebig, and all its many offshoots, may serve you—and serve you well. But if you be a woman of feeling, of fancy, of imagination, for this emergency alone will you reserve your Liebig Who would eat tinned pineapple when the fresh fruit is to be had? Would you give bottled tomatoes preference when the gay *pommes d'amour*, just picked, ornament every stall in the market? Beef extract in skilful hands may work wonders; the soup made from it may deceive the connoisseur of great repute. But what then? Have you no conscience, no respect for your art, that you would thus deceive?

Tinned soups also there be in infinite variety, ox-tail, and mock-turtle, and *Julienne*, and gravy, and chicken broth, and many more than one likes to think of. But dire indeed must be your need before you have recourse to them. They, too, will answer in the hour of want. But at the best, they prove but make-shifts, but paltry make-believes to be avoided, even as you steer clear of the soup vegetables and herbs—bits of carrot and onion and turnip and who knows what?—bottled ingeniously, pretty to the eye, without flavour to the palate. One does not eat to please the sense of sight alone!

When, heroically, you have forsworn the ensnaring tin and the insinuating bottle, the horizon widens before you. "Thick and clear": the phrase suggests but narrow compass; broad beyond measure is the sphere it really opens.

Of all the Doges of Bobbio, but one—if tradition be true—sickened of his hundred soups. Three hundred and sixty-five might have been their number with results no more disastrous. Given a cook of good instincts and gay imagination, and from one year's end to the other never need the same soup be served a second time.

A word, first, as to its proper place on the *menu*. The conservative Briton might think this a subject upon which the last word long since had been spoken. If soup at all, then must it appear between *hors d'œuvre* and fish: as well for Catholic to question the doctrine of infallibility as for self-respecting man to doubt the propriety of this arrangement. But they don't know everything down in Great Britain, and other men there be of other minds. Order a dinner in the American West, and a procession of smiling, white-robed blacks—talking, alas! no more the good old darkey, but pure American—swoop down upon you, bringing at once, in disheartening medley, your blue-points, your gumbo, your terrapin, your reed birds, and your apple pie. What sacrilege! In the pleasantest little restaurant in all Rome, close to the Piazza Colonna, within sound of the Corso, was once to be seen any evening in the week— may be still, for that matter—a bemedalled major finishing his dinner with his *minestra* instead of his *dolce*. But if a fat, little grey-haired man once consent to wear a coat scarce longer than an Eton jacket, may not, in reason, worse enormities be expected of him? Truth to tell, the British convention, borrowed from France, is the best. If, in good earnest, you would profit by your *potage*, give it place of honour at the top of the *menu*. Leave light and frivolous sweets to lighter, more frivolous moments, when, hunger appeased, man may unbend to trifles.

What the great Alexandre calls the *grand consommé* is the basis of all soup—and sauce making. Study his very word with reverence; carry out his every suggestion with devotion. Among the ingredients of this consummate *bouillon* his mighty mind runs riot. Not even the adventures of the immortal Musketeers stimulated his fancy to wilder flights. His directions, large and lavish as himself, would the economical housewife read with awe and something of terror. Veal and beef and fowl—a venerable cock will answer—and rabbit and partridges of yester-year; these be no more than the foundation. Thrown into the *marmite* in fair and fitting proportions, then must they be watched, anxiously and intelligently, as they boil; spoonfuls of the common *bouillon* should be poured upon them from time to time; there must be added onions and carrots, and celery and parsley, and whatever aromatic herbs may be handy, and oil, if you have it; and after four hours of boiling slowly and demurely over a gentle fire, and, next, straining through coarse linen, you may really begin to prepare your soup.

If to these heights the ordinary man—or woman—may not soar, then will the good, substantial, everyday *bouillon*, or *pot-au-feu*—made of beef alone, but ever flavoured with vegetables—fulfil the same purpose, not so deliciously, but still fairly well. In households where soup is, as it should be, a daily necessity, stock may be made and kept for convenience. But if you would have your *pot-au-feu* in perfection, let the saucepan, or *marmite*—the English word is commonplace, the French term charms—be not of iron, but of earthenware: rich tawny brown or golden green in colour, as you see it in many a French market-place, if the least feeling for artistic fitness dwells within your soul Seven hours are needed *pour faire sourire le pot-au-feu*—the expression is not to be translated. Where soups are concerned the English language is poor, and cold, and halting; the speech of France alone can honour them aright.

With good *bouillon* there is naught the genius may not do. Into it the French *chef* puts a few small slices of bread, and, as you eat, you wonder if terrapin or turtle ever tasted better. With the addition of neatly-chopped carrots and onions, and turnips and celery, you have *Julienne;* or, with dainty asparagus tops, sweet fresh peas, tiny stinging radishes, delicate young onions, *printanier*, with its suggestions of spring and blossoms in every mouthful. This last, surely, is the lyric among soups. Decide upon cheese instead, and you will set a Daudet singing you a poem in prose: "*Oh! la bonne odeur de soupe au fromage!*" *Pâtes d'Italie, vermicelli, macaroni*, each will prove a separate ecstasy, if you but remember the grated Parmesan that must be sprinkled over it without stint—as in Italy. Days there be when nothing seems so in keeping as rice: others, when cabbage hath charm, that is, if first in your simmering *bouillon* a piece of ham—whether of York, of Strasbourg, or of Virginia—be left for three hours or more; again, to thicken the golden liquid with tapioca may seem of all devices the most adorable. And so may you ring the changes day after day, week after week, month after month.

If of these lighter soups you tire, then turn with new hope and longing to the stimulating list of *purées* and *crèmes*. Let tomatoes, or peas, or beans, or lentils, as you will, be the keynote, always you may count upon a harmony inspiriting and divine; a rapture tenfold greater if it be enjoyed in some favourite corner at Marguery's or Voisin's, where the masterpiece awaits the chosen few. Or if, when London fogs are heavy and life proves burdensome, comfort is in the very name of broth, then put it to the test in its mutton, Scotch, chicken, or dozen and more varieties, and may it give you new courage to face the worst!

But if for pleasure solely you eat your soup, as you should, unless illness or the blue devils have you firm in their grasp, a few varieties there be which to all the rest are even as is the rose to lesser flowers, as is the onion to vegetables of more prosaic virtue. Clams are a joy if you add to them but salt and pepper—cay-

enne by preference—and a dash of lemon juice·
as a chowder, they are a substantial dream to
linger over; but made into soup they reach
the very topmost bent of their being: it is the
end for which they were created. Of oysters
this is no less true. Veal stock or mutton broth
may pass as prosaic basis of the delicacy; but
better depend upon milk and cream, and of the
latter be not sparing. Mace, in discreet measure, left flowing in the liquid will give the
finishing, the indispensable touch. Oh, the
inexhaustible resources of the sea! With these
delights rank *bisque*, that priceless *purée*, made
of crayfish—in this case a pinch of allspice
instead of mace—and if in its fullest glory you
would know it, go eat it at the Lapérouse on
the Quai des Grands Augustins; eat it, as from
the window of the low room in the *entresol*, you
look over toward the towers of Notre Dame.

Be a good Catholic on Fridays, that, with
potages maigres—their name, too, is legion—
your soups may be increased and multiplied,
and thus infinity become your portion.

THE SIMPLE SOLE

Have you ever considered the sole · the simple, unassuming sole, in Quaker-like garb, striking a quiet grey note in every fishmonger's window, a constant rebuke to the mackerel that makes such vain parade of its green audacity, of the lobster that flaunts its scarlet boldness in the face of the passer-by? By its own merits the sole appeals; upon no meretricious charm does it base its claim for notice Flat and elusive, it seems to seek retirement, to beg to be forgotten. And yet, year by year, it goes on, unostentatiously and surely increasing in price; year by year, it establishes, with firm hold, its preeminence upon the *menu* of every well-regulated *table d'hôte*.

But here pause a moment, and reflect. For it is this very *table d'hôte* which bids fair to be the sole's undoing. If it has been maligned and misunderstood, it is because, swaddled in bread-crumbs, fried in indifferent butter, it has come to be the symbol of hotel or *pension* dinner, until the frivolous and heedlesss begin to believe that it cannot exist otherwise, that in its irrepressible bread-crumbs it must swim through the silent sea.

The conscientious *gourmand* knows better, however He knows that bread-crumbs and frying-pan are but mere child's play compared to its diviner devices. It has been said that the number and various shapes of fishes are not "more strange or more fit for contemplation than their different natures, inclinations, and actions." But fitter subject still for the contemplative, and still more strange, is their marvellous, well-nigh limitless, culinary ambition. Triumph after triumph the most modest of them all yearns to achieve, and if this sublime yearning be ever and always suppressed and thwarted and misdoubted, the fault lies with dull, plodding, unenterprising humans. Not one yearns to such infinite purpose as the sole; not one is so snubbed and enslaved. A very Nora among fish, how often must it long to escape and to live its own life—or, to be more accurate, to die its own death!

Not that bread-crumbs and frying-pan are not all very well in their way. Given a discreet cook, pure virginal butter, a swift fire, and a slice of fresh juicy lemon, something not far short of perfection may be reached. But other ways there are, more suggestive, more inspiring, more godlike. Turn to the French *chef* and learn wisdom from him.

First and foremost in this glorious repertory comes *sole à la Normande*, which, under another name, is the special distinction and pride of the Restaurant Marguery. Take your sole—from the waters of Dieppe would you have the best—and place it, with endearing, lover-like caress, in a pretty earthenware dish, with butter for only companion. At the same time, in sympathetic saucepan, lay mussels to the number of two dozen, opened and well cleaned, as a matter of course; and let each rejoice in the society of a stimulating mushroom; when almost done, but not quite, make of them a garland round the expectant sole; cover their too seductive beauty with a rich white sauce; rekindle their passion in the oven for a few minutes; and serve immediately and hot. Joy is the result; pure, uncontaminated joy. If this be too simple for your taste, then court elaboration and more complex sensation after this fashion: from the first, unite the sole to two of its most devoted admirers, the oyster and the mussel—twelve, say, of each—and let thyme and fragrant herbs and onion and white wine and truffles be close witnesses of their union. Seize the sole when it is yet but half cooked; stretch it out gently in another dish, to which oysters and mussels must follow in hot, precipitate flight. And now the veiling sauce, again white, must have calf's kidney and salt pork for foundation, and the first gravy of the fish for fragrance and seasoning. Mushrooms and lemon in slices may be added to the garniture. And if at the first mouthful you do not thrill with rapture, the Thames will prove scarce deep and muddy enough to hide your shame.

Put to severest test, the love of the sole for the oyster is never betrayed. Would you be convinced—and it is worth the trouble—experiment with *sole farcie aux huîtres*, a dish so perfect that surely, like manna, it must have come straight from Heaven. In prosaic practical language, it is thus composed: you stuff your sole with forcemeat of oysters and truffles, you season with salt and carrot and lemon, you steep it in white wine—not sweet, or the sole is dishonoured—you cook it in the oven, and you serve the happy fish on a rich *ragoût* of the oysters and truffles. Or, another tender conceit that you may make yours to your own great profit and enlightenment, is *sole farcie aux crevettes*. In this case it is wise to fillet the sole and wrap each fillet about the shrimps, which have been well mixed and pounded with butter. A rich *Béchamel* sauce and garniture of lemons complete a composition so masterly that, before it, as before a fine Velasquez, criticism is silenced.

Sole au gratin, though simpler, is none the less desirable. Let your first care be the sauce, elegantly fashioned of butter and mushrooms and shallots and parsley; pour a little—on your own judgment you have best rely for exact quantity—into a baking-dish; lay the sole upon this liquid couch; deluge it with the remainder of the sauce, exhilarating white wine, and lemon juice; bury it under bread-crumbs, and bake it until it rivals a Rembrandt in richness and splendour.

In antiquarian moments, *fricasey soals white*, and admit that your foremothers were more accomplished artists than you. What folly to boast of modern progress when, at table, the Englishman of to-day is but a brute savage compared with his ancestors of a hundred years and more ago! But take heart: be humble, read this golden book, and the day of emancipation cannot be very far distant. Make your *fricasey* as a step in the right direction. According to the infallible book, "skin, wash, and gut your soals very clean, cut off their heads, dry them in a cloth, then with your knife very carefully cut the flesh from the bones and fins on both sides. Cut the flesh long ways, and then across, so that each soal will be in eight pieces; take the heads and bones, then put them into a saucepan with a pint of water, a bundle of sweet herbs, an onion, a little whole pepper, two or three blades of mace, a little salt, a very little piece of lemon peel, and a little crust of bread Cover it close, let it boil till half is wasted, then strain it through a fine sieve, put it into a stew-pan, put in the soals and half a pint of white wine, a little parsley chopped fine, a few mushrooms cut small, a piece of butter as big as an hen's egg, rolled in flour, grate a little nutmeg, set all together on the fire, but keep shaking the pan all the while till the fish is done enough. Then dish it up, and garnish with lemon." And now, what think you of that?

If for variety you would present a brown *fricasey*, an arrangement in browns as startling as a poster by Lautrec or Anquetin, add anchovy to your seasoning, exchange white wine for red, and introduce into the mixture truffles and morels, and mushrooms, and a spoonful of catchup. The beauty of the colour none can deny; the subtlety of the flavour none can resist.

Another step in the right direction, which is the old, will lead you to sole pie, a dish of parts Eels must be used, as is the steak in a pigeon's pie for instance; and nutmeg and parsley and anchovies must serve for seasoning. It is a pleasant fancy, redolent of the days gone by.

"BOUILLABAISSE";

A Symphony in Gold

HEAR Wagner in Baireuth (though illusions may fly like dust before a March wind), see Velasquez in Madrid; eat *Bouillabaisse* in Marseilles And eat, moreover, with no fear of disenchantment; the saffron's gold has richer tone, the *ail's* aroma sweeter savour, under hot blue southern skies than in the cold sunless north.

How much Thackeray is swallowed with your *Bouillabaisse?* asks the cynical American, vowed to all eternity to his baked shad and soft-shelled crab; how much Thackeray? echoes the orthodox Englishman, whose salmon, cucumberless, smacks of heresy, and whose whiting, if it held not its tail decorously in its bread-crumbed mouth, would be cast for ever into outer darkness. Sentiment there may be: not born, however, of Thackeray's verse, but of days spent in Provençal sunshine, of banquets eaten at Provençal tables. Call for *Bouillabaisse* in the Paris restaurant, at the Lapérouse or Marguery's (you might call for it for a year and a day in London restaurants and always in vain); and if the dish brought back something of the true flavour, over it is cast the glamour and romance of its far southern home, of the land of troubadours and of Tartarin. But order it in Marseilles, and the flavour will all be there, and the sunshine and the gaiety, and the song as well; fact outstrips the imagination of even the meridional; the present defies memory to outdo its charm.

And it must be in the Marseilles that glitters under midsummer's sun and grows radiant in its light. Those who have not seen Marseilles at this season know it not. The peevish finder of fault raves of drainage and dynamite, of dirt and anarchy. But turn a deaf ear and go to Marseilles gaily and without dread. Walk out in the early morning on the quays; the summer sky is cloudless; the sea as blue as in the painter's bluest dream; the hills but warm purple shadows resting upon its waters. The air is hot, perhaps, but soft and dry, and the breeze blows fresh from over the Mediterranean. Already, on every side, signs there are of the day's coming sacrifice. In sunlight and in shadow are piled high the sea's sweetest, choicest fruits: mussels in their sombre purple shells; lobsters, rich and brown; fish, scarlet and gold and green. Lemons, freshly plucked from near gardens, are scattered among the fragrant pile, and here and there trail long sprays of salt, pungent seaweed. The faint smell of *ail* comes to you gently from unseen kitchens, the feeling of *Bouillabaisse* is everywhere, and tender anticipation illumines the faces of the passers-by. Great is the pretence of activity in the harbour and in the streets; at a glance, mere paltry traffic might seem the city's one and only end. But Marseilles' true mission, the sole reason for its existence, is that man may know how goodly a thing it is to eat *Bouillabaisse* at noon on a warm summer day.

But when the hour comes, turn from the hotel, however excellent; turn from the Provençal version of the Parisian Duval, however cheap and nasty; choose rather the native headquarters of the immortal dish. Under pleasant awning sit out on the pavement, behind the friendly trees in tubs that suggest privacy, and yet hide nothing of the view beyond. For half the joy in the steaming, golden masterpiece is in the background found for it; in the sunlit harbour and forest of masts; in the classic shores where has disembarked so many a hero, from ancient Phenician or Greek, down to valiant Tartarin, with the brave camel that saw him shoot all his lions! A *coup de vin*, and, as you eat, as you watch, with eyes half blinded, the glittering, glowing picture, you begin to understand the meaning of the southern *galéjado*. Your heart softens, the endless beggars no longer beg from you in vain, while only the slenderness of your purse keeps you from buying out every boy with fans or matches, every stray Moor with silly slippers and sillier antimacassars; your imagination is kindled, so that later, at the gay *café*, where still you sit in the open street, as you look at the Turks and sailors, at the Arabs and Lascars, at the Eastern women in trousers and niggers in rags, in a word, at Marseilles' "Congress of Nations," that even Barnum in his most ambitious moments never approached, far less surpassed, you, too, believe that had Paris but its Canebière, it might be transformed into a little Marseilles on the banks of the Seine. So potent is the influence of blessed *Bouillabaisse!*

Or, some burning Sunday, you may rise with the dawn and take early morning train for Martigues, lying, a white and shining barrier, between the Etangs de Berre and Caronte. And there, on its bridges and canal banks, idly watching the fishing-boats, or wandering up and down its olive-clad hill-sides, the morning hours may be gently loafed away, until the Angelus rings a joyful summons to M. Bernard's hotel in the shady *Place* Dark and cool is the spacious dining-room; eager and attentive the bewildered Désirée. Be not a minute late, for M. Bernard's *Bouillabaisse* is justly famed, and not only all Marseilles, but all the country near hastens thither to eat it on Sundays, when it is served in its *édition de luxe.* Pretty Arlésiennes in dainty fichus, cyclists in knickerbockers, rich Marseillais, painters from Paris join in praise and thanksgiving. And from one end of the world to the other, you might journey in vain in search of an emotion so sweet as that aroused by the first fragrant fumes of the dish set before you, the first rapturous taste of the sauce-steeped bread, of the strange fish so strangely seasoned.

But why, in any case, remain content with salmon alone when *Bouillabaisse* can be made, even in dark and sunless England? Quite the same it can never be as in the land of sunburnt mirth and jollity. The light and the brilliancy and the gaiety of its background must be ever missing in the home of fog and spleen. The gay little fish of the Mediterranean never swim in the drear, unresponsive waters that break on the white cliffs of England and the stern rocks of the Hebrides. But other fish there be, in great plenty, that, in the absence of the original, may answer as praiseworthy copies.

After all, to cut turbot and whiting and soles and trout in small pieces, to cook them all together, instead of each separately, is not the unpardonable sin, however the British housewife may protest to the contrary. And as to the other ingredients, is not good olive oil sold in bottles in many a London shop? Are sweet herbs and garlic unknown in Covent Garden? Are there no French and Italian grocers in Soho, with whom saffron is no less a necessity than mustard or pepper? And bread? who would dare aver that England has no bakers?

It is not a difficult dish to prepare. Its cooks may not boast of secrets known only to themselves, like the maker of process blocks or patent pills. Their methods they disclose without reservation, though alas! their genius they may not so easily impart. First of all, then, see to your sauce: oil, pure and sweet, is its foundation; upon *ail* and herbs of the most aromatic it depends for its seasoning. In this, place your fish selected and mixed as fancy prompts; a whiting, a sole—filleted of course—a small proportion of turbot, and as much salmon, if solely for the touch of colour it gives—the artist never forgets to appeal to the eye as to the palate. Boil thoroughly, sprinkling at the last moment sympathetic saffron on the sweet-smelling offering. Have ready thick slices of bread daintily arranged in a convenient dish; just before serving pour over them the greater part of the unrivalled sauce, now gold and glorious with its saffron tint; pour the rest, with the fish, into another dish—a bowl, would you be quite correct—and let as few seconds as possible elapse between dishing this perfect work of art and eating it. Upon its smell alone man might live and thrive. Its colour is an inspiration to the painter, the subtlety of its flavour a text to the poet Montenard and Dauphin may go on, year after year, painting olive-lined roads and ports of Toulon: the true Provençal artist will be he who fills his canvas with the radiance and richness of *Bouillabaisse*.

Would you emulate M. Bernard and make a *Bouillabaisse de luxe* it may prove a tax upon your purse, but not upon your powers. For when thus lavishly inclined, you but add lobster or crab or crayfish and the needed luxury is secured. It is a small difference in the telling, but in the eating, how much, how unspeakable is this little more! Easily satisfied indeed must be the prosaic mortal who, having once revelled in *Bouillabaisse de luxe*, would ever again still his cravings with the simpler arrangement.

THE MOST EXCELLENT OYSTER

IF, in cruel December, the vegetable fails us, in another direction we may look for and find —if we be wise and liberal—novelty without stint. From the oyster, when it is understood aright, spring perpetual joy and rapturous surprises. But, sad to tell, in England men have slighted it and misdoubted its greatness. Englishmen eat it and declare it good; but, as with salad, they know not how to prepare it. Because it is excellent in its rawness, they can imagine no further use for it, unless, perhaps, to furnish a rich motive for sauce, or sometimes for soup. Even raw—again like salad—they are apt to brutalise it. To drown it in vinegar is the height of their ambition; an imperial pint was the quantity needed by Mr. Weller's friend to destroy the delicacy of its flavour, the salt sweetness of its aroma. The Greeks knew better: according to Athenæus, boiled and fried they served their oysters, finding them, however, best of all when roasted in the coals till the shells opened. As early as the seventeenth century, the French, preparing them *en étuvée* and *en fricassée*, included them in their *Délices de la campagne*. The American to-day exhausts his genius for invention in devising rare and cunning methods by which to extract their full strength and savour. Why should Englishmen tarry behind the other peoples on the earth in paying the oyster the tribute of sympathetic appreciation?

Its merit when raw, no man of sensibility and wisdom will deny. Base-minded, indeed, must be he who thinks to enhance its value by converting it into a defence against influenza or any other human ill. The ancients held it indigestible unless cooked; but to talk of it as if it were a drug for our healing, a poison for our discomforting, is to dishonour, without rhyme or reason, the noblest of all shell-fish. Who would not risk an indigestion, or worse, for the pleasure raw oysters have it in their power to give? Was there one, among the wedding guests at the "Marriage of Hebe," who feared the course of "oysters with closed shells, which are very difficult to open but very easy to eat"?

Easy to eat, yes; but first you must decide which, of the many varieties of oyster the sea offers, you had best order for your own delight. There are some men who, with Thackeray, rank the "dear little juicy green oysters of France" above the "great white flaccid natives in England, that look as if they had been fed on pork." To many, the coppery taste of this English native passes for a charm—poor deluded creatures! To others it seems the very abomination of desolation. But the true epicure, who may not have them, as had oyster-loving Greeks of old, from Abydus or Chalcedon, will revel most of all in the American species: the dainty little Blue-Point, or its long, sweet, plump brother of the north—to swallow it was like swallowing a baby, Thackeray thought.

Once your oysters are on the half shell, let not the vinegar bottle tempt you; as far as it is concerned, be not only temperate, but a total abstainer. A sprinkling of salt, a touch of Cayenne, a dash of lemon juice, and then eat, and know how good it is for man to live in a world of oysters. For a light lunch or the perfect midnight supper, for an inspiring *hors d'œuvre*, without rival is this king of shell-fish. If for the midnight meal you reserve it, you may be kindled into ecstasy by the simple addition of a glass of fine old Chablis or Sauterne —be not led astray by vulgar praise of stout or porter—and brown bread and butter cut in slices of ethereal thinness. Linger over this banquet, exquisite in its simplicity, long and lovingly, that later you may sleep with easy conscience and mind at rest.

With raw oysters alone it were folly to remain content. If you would spread a more sumptuous feast, fry the largest, plumpest grown in sea or river, and the gates of earthly paradise will be thrown wide open in the frying. No more familiar cry is there in American restaurants than that for "an oyster fry!" Dark little oyster cellars, reached by precipitous steps, there are, and friendly seedy little oyster shops in back streets, where the frying of oysters has been exalted into a holy cult. And if you will, in paper boxes, the long, beautiful, golden-brown masterpieces you may carry away with you, to eat with gayer garnishing and in more sympathetic surroundings. And in winter, scarce a beer saloon but, at luncheon time, will set upon the counter a steaming dish of fried oysters; and with every glass of no matter what, "crackers" at discretion and one fried oyster on long generous fork will be handed by the white-robed guardian. But mind you take but one: else comes the chucker-out. Thus, only the very thirsty, in the course of a morning, may gain a free lunch. But, in England, what is known of the fried oyster?

It requires no great elaboration, though much rare skill in the cooking. For this purpose the largest oysters must be selected: the fattest and most juicy. In the half-shell they may be fried, after seventeenth-century fashion, a touch of butter and pepper on each; verjuice or vinegar, and grated nutmeg added once they are served. Or else, taken from the shell, they may be dipped into a marvellous preparation of vinegar, parsley, laurel leaves, onion, chives, cloves, basil, and in the result the mighty imagination of the great Alexandre would rejoice. Or, again, in simpler American fashion, enveloped in unpretentious batter of eggs and bread crumbs, fry them until they turn to an unrivalled, indescribable golden-brown, and in the eating thereof the gods might envy you.

If a new sensation you court, grill or broil your oyster, and you will have cause to exult in a loud triumphant *magnificat*. No bread crumbs are needed, neither laurel nor sweet spice. With but a bit of butter for encouragement, it will brown gently in the grilling, and become a delicious morsel to be eaten with reverence and remembered with tenderness.

Or, stew them and be happy. But of rich milk, and cream, and sweet fresh butter, as Dumas would put it, must your stew be made: thickened, but scarce perceptibly, with flour, while bits of mace float in golden sympathy on the liquid's surface. It is the dish for luncheon, or for the pleasant, old-fashioned "high tea"—no such abomination as "meat tea" known then, if you please—of Philadelphia's pleasant, old-fashioned citizens. And a worse accompaniment you might have than waffles, light as a feather, or beaten biscuits, the pride of Maryland's black cooks Men and women from the Quaker city, when in cruel exile, will be moved to sad tears at the very mention of Jones's "oyster stews" in Eleventh-street!

But the glory of Penn's town is the oyster croquette—from Augustine's by preference. A symphony in golden brown and soft fawn grey, it should be crisp without, within of such delicate consistency that it will melt in the mouth like a dream. Pyramidal in shape, it is of itself so decorative that only with the rarest blue and white china, or the most fairy-like Limoges, will it seem in perfect harmony. It would be discourteous, indeed, to serve so regal a creation on any stray dish or plate.

Exquisite pleasure lurks in scalloped oysters, or oysters *au gratin*, whichever you may choose to call this welcome variation of the oyster motive. Layers of judiciously seasoned breadcrumbs alternate with layers of the responsive shell-fish, and the carefully-studied arrangement is then browned until it enchants by colour no less than by fragrance. And, if you would seek further to please the eye, let the dish to hold so fine a work of art be a shell, with a suggestion of the sea in its graceful curves and tender tints. Or, if imagination would be more daring, let the same shell hold *huîtres farcies*, cunningly contrived with eels and oysters, and parsley and mushrooms, and spices and cream, and egg and aromatic herbs. So fantastic a contrivance as this touches upon sublimity.

In more homely and convivial mood, roast your oysters, as the Greeks loved them. But to enjoy them to the utmost, roast them yourself in the coals of your own fire, until the ready shells open. A dash of salt and cayenne upon the sweet morsel within, and you may eat it at once, even as you take it from off the coals, and drink its salt, savoury liquor from the shell. A dish of anchovy toast will not seem amiss. But let no other viands coarsen this ideal supper. For supper it should be, and nothing else. The curtains must be drawn close, while the fire flames high; one or two congenial friends—not more; a dim religious light from well-shaded lamps and candles; a bottle of good old Chablis, and others waiting in near wine-cellar or sideboard; and thus may you make your own such unspeakable happiness as seldom falls to the lot of mortals.

Or if to the past your fancy wanders, prepare your oysters, seventeenth century-fashion, *en étuvée*, boiled in their own liquor, flavoured with ingredients so various as oranges and chives, and served with bread-crumbs; or else, *en fricassée*, cooked with onion and butter, dipped in batter, and sprinkled with orange juice. Or again, in sheer waywardness, curry or devil them, though in this disguise no man may know the delicacy he is eating. Another day, bake them; the next, put them in a pie or a patty, the third, let them give substance to a *vol-au-vent*. Hesitate at no experiment; search the cookery-books, old and new. Be sure that the oyster, in its dictionary, knows no such word as fail. If in sheer recklessness you were, like young Mr Grigg in the Cave of Harmony, to call for a "mashed oyster and scalloped 'taters," no doubt the "mashed" would be forthcoming.

As basis of soup or sauce, the oyster is without rival. Who would not abstain on Fridays all the year round, if every Friday brought with it oyster soup to mortify the flesh! But alas! four months there be without an R, when oysters by the wise must not be eaten. And is not turbot, or boiled capon, or a tender loin-steak but the excuse for oyster sauce? in which, if you have perfection for your end, let there be no stint of oysters. Then, too, in the stuffing of a fowl, oysters prove themselves the worthy rival of mushrooms or of chestnuts.

It is a grave mistake, however, to rank the oyster as the only shellfish of importance. The French know better. So did the Greeks, if Athenæus can be trusted. Mussels, oysters, scallops, and cockles led the list, according to Diocles, the Carystian. Thus are they enumerated by still another authority:—

> A little polypus, or a small cuttle-fish,
> A crab, a crawfish, oysters, cockles,
> Limpets and solens, mussels and pinnas;
> Periwinkles, too, from Mitylene.

The mussel is still the delight of the French *table d'hôte* breakfast. Charming to look at is the deep dish where, floating in parsley-strewn sauce, the beautiful purple shells open gently to show the golden-grey treasures within. Well may the commercial in the provinces heap high his plate with the food he loves, while about him hungry men stare, wondering how much will be left for their portion. But who in England eats mussels? Only a little lower the Greeks ranked periwinkles, which now, associated as they are with 'Arriet and her pin, the fastidious affect to despise. It has been written of late, by a novelist seeking to be witty, that there is no poetry in periwinkles; but Æschylus could stoop to mention them in his great tragedies. The "degradation of the lower classes" the same weak wit attributes to overindulgence in winkles. With as much reason might the art and philosophy of Greece be traced to "periwinkles from Mitylene." Cooked in the good sauce of France, the humble winkle might take rank with the Whitstable native at three-and-six the dozen, and thus would the lowly be exalted. The snail, likewise, we might cultivate to our own immeasurable advantage.

THE PARTRIDGE

With September, the *gourmand's* fancy gaily turns to thoughts of partridges. For his pleasure sportsmen, afar in autumn's cool country, work diligently from morn to eve; or, it may be, he himself plays the sportsman by day that he may prove the worthier *gourmand* by night. And the bird is deserving of his affections It has been honoured alike in history and romance.

Among moderns, a Daudet is found to study and consider its emotions under fire; among ancients, few neglected it, from Aristophanes to Aristotle, who declared it "a very ill-disposed and cunning animal; much devoted, moreover, to amatory enjoyment." With such a character, its two hearts count for little; far gone, indeed, must be the sentimentalist of our moral age who would stay its slayer's hand. What if it be true, as Chamæleon of Pontus said of old, that from listening to its singing in desert places man arrived at the art of music?

Alive it may have an æsthetic value; but if it be without morals should it not perish? In eating it, therefore, does not man perform a solemn duty? Nay, should not the New Woman exult in flaunting its sober feathers in her masculine hat?

So might reason the apostle of social purity. But the *gourmand* questions nothing save the daintiness of the bird's flesh, the merit of its flavour. And the practical answer to this questioning silences all doubts Clearly the partridge was created that he might eat it and find it good

It is because of the rare excellence of the pretty bird, in autumn making a feathered frieze in every poulterer's window, that too much consideration cannot be given to its treatment in the kitchen. Its virtues can be easily marred by the indifferent, or unsympathetic *chef*. Left hanging too short a time, left cooking too long, and it will sink into commonplace, so that all might wonder wherefore its praises have been ever loudly sung. Hang it in a cool place, and leave it there until the last moment possible—you understand? Now that winds are cold, and a feeling of frost is in the air, to banish it a fortnight would not be unwise.

To roast a partridge may seem a sadly simple device when so many more ingenious schemes are at your disposal. But for all that, none can be recommended with enthusiasm more keenly felt. For in the roasting none of its sweet savour is lost, none of its natural tenderness sacrificed on the one hand, exaggerated on the other. The process requires less intelligence than an artistic touch. Truss your birds in seemly fashion, when, as if in birdlike emulation of Hedda Gabler, they cry for vine leaves on their breast. Over the vine leaves tie less romantic, but more succulent, bacon, cut in slices of the thinnest. Then, in front of a quick, clear fire baste prodigally with butter. A little flour, judiciously sprinkled, will add richness to the nut-brown colour the susceptible birds develop in the roasting. Now they are ready to serve, remember that "partridges should have gravy in the dish, and bread-sauce in a cup"—it is Mrs Glasse who has said it. It would be no crime to add watercress, or parsley, as garniture, or toast as a soft bed for the happy victims. And to eat with them, prepare a crisp lettuce salad, to which the merest suspicion of tarragon leaves, well chopped, has been added. And the gods themselves might envy you your joy and gladness in the eating.

A word as to the carving, or "dissection of the partridge," as it was called in days when England understood and gloried in the arts of the kitchen. Thus was the *Grand Escuyer Tranchant*—the Great Master carver, that is—instructed: "A partridge is for the most part carved and served whole, like a pigeon; but yet he may be served in pieces; but when you will carve him to serve whole, you must only cut the joints and lay them abroad; but if you serve him by pieces, you must begin to serve with a wing." Why not carve and serve according to tradition, and so lend new dignity to your feasting?

If of roast partridge you weary, and from France would take a hint, seek novelty and happiness in *Perdrix aux choux* For this, birds of an older generation will answer as well as their more tender young, since for two hours, in a wrapping of bacon and buttered paper, they must simmer gently on their couch of cabbage. To evolve the required flavour, into the same pot must go a saveloy, and perhaps salt pork in slices, a bunch of fragrant herbs, onions and carrots and cloves and salt and butter *à discrétion.* The birds must be drained before they pass from the pot to the dish; around them the cabbage, likewise drained, must be set as a garland, and the saveloy, in pretty pieces, may be placed here and there. Behold another of the many good gifts France has presented to us.

Perdrix à l'Espagnole may again vary anew the delicious monotony. In this variety the partridges are boiled, covered with a rich gravy, and plentifully adorned with green peppers. It was in a moment of divine inspiration the Spaniard invented so piquant an arrangement But the resources of boiled partridges, apt to be forgotten or overlooked, are well-nigh limitless, and as charming as they are many. Very important is it that the birds be well boiled, quickly, in much water. The rest depends upon the sauce. This may be of cream and butter alone; or else of celery and cream, seasoned with mace and pepper. Or else of mushrooms and cream, or of the livers and parsley and butter; or of white wine; or of any and every good thing that goes to the making of superlative sauce. What a chance, too, to exercise your imagination, to reveal your ingenuity! Five long months are before you; see that you make the most of them.

If your soul delight in the fantastic, let few days pass before you have tested the quaint joys of *Partridge Mettenes*. The recipe shall be printed word for word as written by the Master Cook, Giles: "Take Partridges and roast them, then take Cream"—these with capitals, observe—"and Grapes, with Bread, scorched against the Fire, and beat all this together; but first steep your Bread in Broth or Claret-Wine; then strain all this through a strainer with Spice, Cinnamon, and a little Mustard; set all a-boyling with a pretty deal of Sugar, but take heed that it doth not burn too, and when you would serve away your Partridge, put them into a Dish, and your Sauce under them, and garnish your Dish with Sweetmeats and Sugar-plumbs."

Here is another device, fantastic chiefly in name: "Partridges *à l'eau béniste* or Holy Water." It has the virtue of simplicity. "Take partridges and rost them, and when they are rosted, cut them into little pieces, and put them into a Dish with a little fair Water and Salt, and make them boyl a little, and so serve them away." Or else, O pleasant alternative! "you may make a Sauce with Rose-water and Wine, the Juice of Apples and Oranges, but there must be three times as much Rose-water as Wine."

Reading this, who will dare deny that Master Cook Giles is an authority to be respected, of whose recipes the poor prosaic modern kitchen may not receive too many? Space, therefore, must be yielded to at least one more: "Partridges à la Tonnelette." "Take a partridge and rost it, then put it into a Pot; this done, take white Bread and scorch or toste it very brown, but not burn it, and put it a-steeping in good Claret-wine, and when it is well steep'd strain it through a strainer with some good Broth, and a few Onions fryed in Lard, with a little Cinnamon, Cloves, and Nutmegs, and other small Spices, and a little Sugar, and put into it a handful of Currants, and make that which you have strained out boyl all together, and when it is time to serve your Partridges, put your Sauces into a Dish, and lay your Partridges upon it, and so serve it."

Such pretty fancies, it were a shame to follow with bald prose. Yet, bear in mind that partridges may be braised with mushrooms or truffles; that they may be broiled or baked; that they disgrace neither pie nor pudding; and that they offer welcome basis for a *salmi* and *purée*. Lay this to heart.

THE ARCHANGELIC BIRD

MICHAELMAS is a season of sad associations. The quarter's rent is due, alas! The quarter's gas, alas! and, alas a hundred times! the half-yearly rates. Bank accounts dwindle; spirits sink; life seems but a blank and dreary desert.

Into the gloom, settling down thicker and more throttling than November's fog, there flutters and waddles a big white bird, a saviour of men. It is the noble goose, the goose, ridiculed and misunderstood, that comes chivalrously and fearlessly to the rescue; the goose that once saved Rome's Capitol, the goose still honoured as most alert of sentinels within Barcelona's cathedral precincts, the goose that, followed by a goose-girl, is the beloved of artists. Because of its nobility of character, its devotion, wherein it rivals benevolent mastiff and kindly terrier, its courage, its strength, St Michael, glorious and effulgent archangel, took it for his own bird of birds, to be so intimately connected with him that now to show respect to the Saint is to eat the goose. The Feast of Michaelmas, to the right-minded and the orthodox, means roast goose and apple sauce. Soulless authorities, burrowing in mouldy records, can find no better reason for this close relationship than that, at September's close, great is the number of geese cackling in homely barnyard, great their perfection. Numerous generations since England's fourth Edward sat upon the throne (and who can say how many before his time?), have held the cooking of the goose for dinner as no less sacred a ceremony on the Angel's feast day than the morning's service in church. And this, would the pugnacious Michael have permitted for such gross material considerations? Never; let it be said once and for all: never. He knew the goose for the bird that lays the golden egg; he knew full well its dignity and might that make it still a terror to be met on lonely common by them who use its name as symbol of silliness; he knew that strong as well as faint hearted hesitate to say "Bo" discourteously to any goose, whether it be a wanderer in French pastures or

The Archangelic Bird

one of the dust-raising flock, in the twilight, cackling homeward over Transylvanian highways. In a word, Michael knew his bird; and our duty it is to believe in it a dish for Michaelmas with the blind, unquestioning allegiance of perfect faith. Coarse its flesh may be in comparison with the dainty duck and tender chicken; commonplace in comparison with the glorious grouse and proud partridge. The modest, respectable *bourgeois* it may seem among poultry. And yet, if the Archangel has chosen it for his own, who shall say him nay? Study rather to disguise its native coarseness, to enliven its excellent dulness.

To roast it is the simplest form the Michaelmas celebration allows See first that your fire be very good; take care to singe the sacrificial goose with a piece of white paper, and baste it with a piece of butter; drudge it (the word is Mrs Glasse's) with a little flour, and when the smoke begins to draw to the fire, and it looks plump, baste it again and drudge it with a little flour, and take it up In sober mood, stuff it with sage and onion; in more flamboyant moments, let your choice rest upon chestnuts.

Tradition insists upon a little good gravy in a basin by itself, and some apple-sauce in another; but sauce of gooseberries, not to be had fresh, however, for Michaelmas, is the *gourmet's* choice.

A hint as to carving. How many a beautiful bird, or majestic joint, has been shamelessly insulted by ill-trained carver! Of old the master of the household accepted the "dissection of a goose" after the High Dutch fashion and the Italian both, his own predilections leaning rather toward the High Dutch, "for they cut the breast into more pieces, and so by consequence fill more Plates"—good thrifty burghers that they were. Learn then, and master "the order how they carve and how they send it away; as (1), on the first Plate a thigh; (2), another thigh; (3), a side of the rump, with a piece of the breast; (4), the other side of the rump, with another piece of the breast; (5), a wing; (6), the other wing; (7), the rest of the stomach, upon which, if there be little of the brawn left, you may joyn the two small forked bones; to the eighth, the merry-thought, with the rest of the rump, and any else, at your discretion. If you will, you may join some of the breast with the best piece which you always present to the most considerable person at the table first, and take notice too, by the bye, the brawn of the breast ought to be for the most part served out first." Give heed unto these directions, and far wrong you may not go.

Days are when simple expression of faith is all too inadequate The devout yearns for something more ornate, something more elaborate. Let the outcome of this yearning be *oie à la chipolata*, and Michael in Paradise will smell the sweet savour and smile. It is difficult, but delicious. Cover the bottom of your stew-pan with lard; place upon it two or three slices of beef and ham, a bouquet of parsley and chives, three carrots and two or three onions, a touch of garlic, a few cloves, thyme, laurel leaves, basil, and salt, and thus you will have prepared a sweet, soft bed for your goose. Immediately disturb the bird's slumbers by pouring over it a glass of good Madeira, a bottle of white wine, a glass of cognac, and two or three spoonfuls of strong bouillon made of fowls.

Now put your pan on the fire, stew your goose for an hour, lift it out, arrange it on a fair dish, and envelop it in the very richest *chipolata* it is in your power to make. And what is a *chipolata?* An Italian creation half sauce, half *ragoût,* fashioned of carrots and turnips, and chestnuts and onions, and sausage and mushrooms, and artichokes and celery, and strong veal gravy.

Archangelic smiles must broaden into silent laughter at the mere mention of "a Potage of Green Geese." It is a conceit redolent of the olden time, when gaiety was still ranked among the cardinal virtues, and men ate their fill with no fear of a dyspeptic to-morrow. Since it is an ancient masterpiece, in the ancient words must it be explained, or else it will be dishonoured in the telling. "Take your Green-geese and boyl them the usual way, and when they are boyled take them up and fry them whole in a frying-pan to colour them, either with the fat of bacon or hog's-lard, called nowadays *manège de pork;* then take ginger, long pepper, and cloves; beat all this together, and season them with this spice; a little parsley and sage, and put them into a little of the same broth that they were boyled in, and sprinkle a little grated cheese over them, and let them have a little stew, and then dish them up with sipets under them." A brave disguise, truly, for humblest goose.

In a pie likewise—unless the fashioning thereof be entrusted to the indiscreet cook—it presents a brave appearance. Walls of crust line a spacious dish; a pickled dried tongue is boiled; a fowl and a goose are boned; seasoning is wrought of mace, beaten pepper, and salt; and then, Oh the marvel of it! fowl is lain in the goose, tongue in the fowl, goose in the dish. A half a pound of butter separates bird from pastry cover. And, hot or cold, pleasure may be had in the eating. Not the highest pleasure, perhaps, but still pleasure not to be scorned.

If you would boil a goose, see, as you respect your stomach, that it be first salted for a week. With onion sauce it may be becomingly adorned, or again, with simple cabbage, boiled, chopped small, and stewed in butter. Or, plunge gaily into the *rococo* style, and decorate it *à l'Arlé-*

sienne; stuffed with onions and chestnuts, boiled in company with carrots and celery and onions and parsley and cloves, floated in tomato sauce, it is as chock full of playful surprises as the *Cartuja* of Granada. Another device to be recommended is the grilling of the legs and the serving them with *laitues farcies*—and Michael will laugh outright; or *à la Provençale*, and words fail; or *aux tomates*, the love-apples that not the hardest heart can resist. Of the great and good Carême these are the suggestions; treasure them up, therefore, where memory may not rust or aspiration decay, for the dinner may come when you will be glad to have them at hand.

Of the giblets and liver of the goose is there not a long, exultant chapter yet to be written? In far Strasburg geese, in perpetual darkness and torture, fatten with strange morbid fat, that the sensitive, who shrink from a bull fight and cry out against the cruelty of the cockpit, may revel in *pâté de foie gras*. So long as the world lives, may there still be this delectable *pâté* to delight. But why not be honest: admit that between the torture of the bull that we may see, and the torture of the goose that we may eat, difference there is none? Give sensitiveness full play, and sordid vegetarianism is the logical result.

SPRING CHICKEN

GLUTTONY, it has been written — and with wisdom — deserves nothing but praise and encouragement. For two reasons. "Physically, it is the result and proof of the digestive organs being perfect. Morally, it shows implicit resignation to the commands of nature, who, in ordering man to eat that he may live, gives him appetite to invite, flavour to encourage, and pleasure to reward." But there is a third reason, too often overlooked even by the professional glutton: love of good eating is an incentive to thought, a stimulus to the imagination. The man of the most active mind and liveliest fancy is he who eats well and conscientiously considers each dish as it is set before him.

The test seldom fails. Run through the list of poets and painters of your acquaintance; do not they who eat best write the finest verse and paint the strongest pictures? Those who pretend indifference and live on unspeakable messes are betrayed in the foolish affectation and tedious eccentricity of their work; those who feel indifference are already beyond hope and had better far be selling tape across counters or adding up figures in loathsome ledgers Memory, borrowing from her store-house of treasures, lingers with tender appreciation and regret upon one unrivalled breakfast, exquisitely cooked, exquisitely served, and exquisitely eaten, when lilacs were sweet and horse-chestnuts blossoming in the boulevards and avenues of Paris. And he upon whose table the banquet was spread is an artist who towers head and shoulders above the pigmies of his generation. It were rash, indeed, to maintain that because he eats daintily therefore he paints like the master he is; but who, on the other hand, would dare aver that because he paints supremely well therefore is he the prince of *gourmets?* Here cause and effect are not to be defined by cold logic, not to be labelled by barren philosophy. One thing alone is certain; if love of good eating will not create genius it can but develop it.

Consequently, it would be impossible to think too much of what you are eating to-day and purpose to eat to-morrow. It is your duty above all things to see that your food is in harmony with place and season. The question now is, what beast or bird is fitting holocaust for the first warm months of spring? Beef is too heating, too substantial; mutton too monotonous, veal too prosaic. Lamb hath charm, but a charm that by constant usage may be speedily exhausted. Does not mint sauce pall at times? Place, then, your trust in the poultry-yard that your pleasure may be long in the spring.

To begin with, poultry pleases because of its idyllic and pastoral associations. The plucked birds, from shop windows, flaunting their nakedness in the face of the world, recall the old red-roofed farmhouse among the elms, and the pretty farmer's daughter in neat, fresh gingham, scattering grain in the midst of her feathered favourites; they suggest the first cool light of dawn and the irrepressible cock crowing the glad approach of day; in a word, they are reminders of the country's simple joys—

unendurable at the time, dear and sacred when remembered in town.

The gentle little spring chicken is sweet and adorable above all its kindred poultry. It is innocent and guileless as Bellini's angels, dream-like and strange as Botticelli's. It is the very concentration of spring; as your teeth meet in its tender, yielding flesh, you think, whether you will or no, of violets and primroses, and hedgerows white with may; you feel the balmy breath of the south wind; the world is scented for you with lilac and narcissus; and, for the time being, life is a perfect poem. But —why is there always a but?—your cook has it in her power to ruin the rhythm, to make of melodious lyric the most discordant prose. No less depends upon the being who cooks the chicken than upon the hen who laid the egg. If hitherto you have offended through heedlessness, see now that you approach the subject with a determination to profit.

Of all ways of cooking a spring chicken, frying is first to be commended; and of all ways of frying the American is most sympathetic. Fried chicken! To write the word is to be carried back to the sunny South; to see, in the mind's eye, the old, black, fat, smiling *mammie*, in gorgeous bandana turban, and the little black piccaninnies bringing in relays of hot muffins. Oh, the happy days of the long ago! It is easy to give the *recipe*, but what can it avail unless the *mammie* goes with it? Another admirable device is in broiling. One fashion is to divide your chicken down the back and flatten it, seeing, as you have a heart within you, that no bones be broken. Set it lovingly on a trivet placed for the purpose in a baking-tin into which water, to the depth of an inch, has been poured. Cover your tin; bake the sweet offering for ten minutes or so; take it from the oven; touch it delicately with the purest of pure olive oil, and for another ten minutes broil it over a good brisk fire. And if in the result you do not taste heaven, hasten to the hermit's cell in the desert, and, for the remainder of your days, grow thin on lentils and dates.

Or, if you would broil your chicken after the fashion of infallible Mrs Glasse, slit it as before, season it with pepper and salt, lay it on a clear fire at a great distance, broil first the inside, then the out, cover it with delicate breadcrumbs, and let it be of a fine brown, but not burnt. And keep this note carefully in your mind: "You may make just what sauce you fancy."

To roast a spring chicken will do no harm, but let it not be overdone. Twenty minutes suffice for the ceremony. Bacon, in thinnest of thin slices, gracefully rolled, is not unworthy to be served with it. In boiling, something of its virginal flavour may be sacrificed, but still there is compensating gain; it may be eaten with white mushroom sauce, made of mushrooms and cream, and seasoned with nutmeg and mace. Here is a poem, sweeter far than all songs of immortal choirs or the weak pipings of our minor singers.

As the chicken outgrows the childish state, you may go to Monte Carlo in search of one hint at least, for its disposal. There you will learn to cut it into quarters, to stew it in wine and shallots, to add, at the psychological moment, tomatoes in slices, and to serve a dish that baffles description. Or you may journey to Spain, and find that country's kitchen slandered when you eat *poulet au ris à l'Espagnole*, chicken cooked in a *marmite* with rice, artichokes, green and red chillies, and salad oil, and served, where the artist dwells, in the blesssed *marmite* itself—in unimaginative London, even, you may buy one, green or brown, whichever you will, at a delightful shop in Shaftsbury-avenue. Again, you may wander to Holland—it is a short journey, and not disagreeable by way of Harwich—and be ready to swear that no fashion can surpass the Dutch of boiling chickens with rice or vermicelli, spicing them with pepper and cloves, and, at table, substituting for sauce sugar and cinnamon. But to omit these last two garnishments will not mean a mortal sin upon your conscience. In more festive mood hasten at once to France, and there you will be no less certain that the way of ways is to begin to broil your chicken, already quartered, but, when half done, to put it in a stew-pan with gravy, and white wine, salt and pepper, fried veal balls, onions, and shallots, and, according to season, gooseberries or grapes. Do you not grow hungry as you read?

But wait: this is not all. As the beautiful mixture is stewing—on a charcoal fire if possible—thicken the liquor with yolks of eggs and the juice of lemon, and for ever after bless Mrs Glasse for having initiated you into these noble and ennobling mysteries.

Braise your chicken, fricassee it, make it into mince, croquettes, krameskies; eat it cold; convert it into galantine; bury it in aspic; do what you will with it, so long as you do it well, it can bring you but happiness and peace.

THE MAGNIFICENT MUSHROOM

From remote ages dates the triumph of the mushroom—the majestic, magnificent mushroom. Glorious Greeks feasted on it and were glad. What say Poliochus and Antiphanes? What Athenæus? In verse only, could be duly praised those fragrant mushrooms of old, which were roasted for dinner and eaten with delicate snails caught in the dewy morning, and olives tenderly pounded; washed down with wine, good if not over strong or of famous vintage. O the simple, happy days of long ago!

There are times when the classic simplicity and dignity of the Greek you may emulate, and your amusement find in mushrooms dressed with vinegar, or honey and vinegar, or honey, or salt. But then, all other courses must be in keeping. The snails and olives must not be omitted. Maize there must be, well winnowed from the chaff, and rich, ripe purple figs. And, who knows? the full flavour thereof might not be yielded to the most earnest adventurer were couches not substituted for stiff, ungainly chairs. By many a lesser trifle has digestion been, if not ruined, influenced for ill.

But the classic experiment, if repeated too often, might seem very odious. The modern *gourmand*, or artist, is a romanticist, whether he will or no No screaming red waistcoat marks the romantic movement in the kitchen, and yet there it has been stronger even than in art and literature. The picturesque must be had at any cost. Simplicty is not spurned, far from it; but it must be seasoned with becoming sprinkling of romance. What could be simpler than the common mushroom grilled, so self-sufficient in its chaste severity that it allows but salt and pepper and butter to approach it, as it lies, fragrant and delicious, on its gridiron, calling, like another St Lawrence, to be turned when one side is fairly done. And yet when, ready to be served, its rich brown beauty is spread upon the paler brown of the toast, and above rests butter's brilliant gold, have you not an arrangement as romantic in conception as the "Ernani" of the master, or the pastoral of Corot? Paltry meats and undesirable vegetables should not be allowed to dispute supremacy with it. Serve it alone, as you respect yourself. Do not make your breakfast or dinner table as preposterous a blunder as the modern picture gallery.

Should simplicity pall upon you—and moments there are when it cannot fail to pall—enrich your grilled mushrooms with a sauce of melted butter and onions and parsley, and a single note of garlic, and the result will be enchanting mushrooms *à la bourdelaise*. If *au beurre* you would eat them, to accord with your passing mood of suave serenity, stew them gently and considerately in daintiest stewpan your kitchen can provide, and let cayenne and powdered mace exult, as the romantic elements of the stirring poem.

A still more poetic fancy may be met and sweely satisfied by *ragoût* of mushrooms. Listen reverently, for it is food fit to be set before the angels. Over the mushrooms, first boiled on a quick fire, pour a gill of pure red wine—

and the best Burgundy thus used will not be wasted; then scatter spices, mace, and nutmeg, with a discreet hand; boil once more; pour the marvellous mixture upon five or six—or more, if wanted—yolks of eggs, hard-boiled; garnish the dish with grilled mushrooms, and bless the day that you were born, predestined, as you were, from all eternity for this one interval of rapture.

Possibility of rapture there is likewise in a white *fricassée* of mushrooms, which, if you have your own happiness at heart, you cannot afford to despise. Secure then, without delay—for who would play fast and loose with happiness? —a quart of fresh mushrooms. Clean them with hands as tender as if bathing a new-born babe. In three spoonfuls of water, and three of milk, let them boil up three times. See that temptation leads you not to violate the sanctity of this thrice-three. Nutmeg, mace, butter, a pint of rich thick cream alone, at this juncture, will appease the saucepan's longings. Shake well; and all the time, mind you. Be careful there is no curdling, or else—damnation. The masterpiece once triumphantly achieved and set upon a table covered with a fair white cloth, great will be the rejoicing in the Earthly Paradise of your dining-room.

Another sensation, another thrill awaits you in mushrooms *au gratin*. Here, indeed, is romanticism gone mad. Grated bacon, shallots, a *bouquet garni*, mace, pepper and salt, eggs and butter share the baking-dish with the mushrooms; breadcrumbs complete the strange, subtle combination, upon which you may break your fast, dine, sup and sleep, as Valentine upon the very naked name of love. A sorry plight were yours if love, fickle and fading, could be preferred to a dish of mushrooms fashioned so fantastically.

"And oh! what lovely, beautiful eating there is in this world!" It is Heine who said it—Heine who, for a good dinner, would have given twice the three hundred years of eternal fame offered by Voltaire for a good digestion. But lovely and beautiful are but feeble words when it is a question of the mess of mushrooms, for which who would not sacrifice eternal fame for ever, in all cheerfulness and glee?

The reigning sultana in the mushroom's

harem is the brilliant golden egg. Sweet symphonies in brown and gold are the dishes their union yields. *Œufs brouillés aux champignons*—has not the very name a pretty sound? It is a delight best suited to the midday breakfast; a joyous course to follow the anchovy salad, the eel well smoked, or whatever dainty *hors d'œuvre* may stimulate to further appetite. The eggs, scrambled and rivalling the buttercup's rich gold, are laid delicately on crisp toast, and present a couch, soft as down, for a layer of mushrooms. Let Ruskin rave of Turner's sunsets, let the glory of the Venetians be a delight among art critics; but when did Turner or Titian or Tintoret invent a finer scheme of colour than egg and mushroom thus combined for the greater happiness of the few? A silver dish or one of rarest porcelain should be frame for a picture so perfect

Borrow a hint from the Hungarians, and vary the arrangement to your own profit. Make a *purée* of the mushrooms, as rich as cream permits, and offer it as foundation for eggs poached deftly and swiftly: a harmony in soft dove-like greys and pale yellow, the result. It is an admirable contrivance, a credit to Szomorodni-drinking Magyars. And there is no known reason why it should not be eaten on Thames side as on the banks of the Danube. Szomorodni, in its native splendour, alas! is not to be had in London town. But, without sacrilege, Chablis or Graves, or Sauterne may take its place. To drink red wine would be to strike a false note in the harmony.

Another day, another dish, which you cannot do better than make *omelette aux champignons*. And if you will, you may eat it even as it was prepared for Royal Stuarts by Master Cook Rose, who wrote almost as prettily as he cooked. Thus:—" Stove your champignons between two dishes, season them with salt, pepper, and nutmeg, then make an omelette with a dozen of eggs, and when he is ready cover him over with your champignons, and fold him up, triangle-wise, and serve him with the juice of lemons over him." A royal dish, indeed.

Creatures of infinite resources, eggs and mushrooms meet in cases to produce a new and distinct joy. The mushrooms, stewed in milk thickened with the yolks of raw eggs and breadcrumbs, line the little fluted china cases; into each a fresh egg is broken; then more mushrooms and breadcrumbs are spread gently above; a shallow pan, its bottom just covered with hot water, receives the cases, and ten minutes in the oven will complete a triumph which, once tasted, you may well remember all the days of your life.

The kidney is loved by the mushroom scarce less tenderly than the egg. *Rognons aux champignons*, fragrant rich, ravishing, may also be claimed by the happy midday hour. And like so many a noble dish, it lavishes upon you the pleasures of anticipation. For the kidneys, cut in slices and laid in thickened gravy, must stew slowly, slowly—never boiling, unless you would have them vie with leather in consistency. At an early stage the mushrooms, also in pieces, may be added, and pepper and salt according to inclination. And slowly, slowly let the stewing continue. At the last supreme moment pour in a glass of generous red wine, or if it please you more, Marsala, and serve without delay. Chambertin, or Nuits, at peace in its cradle, is surely the wine decreed by fate to drink with so sublime a creation.

With the tender *filet*, mushrooms prove irresistible; with the graceful cutlet they seem so ravishing that even *sauce Soubise*, the once inseparable, may for the moment be easily forgotten. And veal is no less susceptible to its charms: let *noisettes de veau aux champignons* be the *entrée* of to-morrow's dinner, and you will return thanks to your deliverer from the roast!

As sauce, mushroom is the chosen one of fowl and fish alike. Join your mushrooms to *Béchamel*, one of the great mother sauces, and you will have the wonder that Carême, its creator, served first to the Princesse de B. How resist so aristocratic a precedent? *Grasse*, or *maigre*, you can make it, as the season demands. Or to a like end you may devote that other marvel, *purée de champignons à la Laguipierre*, whose patron was the great Louis de Rohan, and into whose mysteries Carême was initiated by the "Grand M. Dunan." Ham, tomato, nutmeg, pepper, lemon juice, are the chief ingredients that enter into its composition. Who, after testing it, will dare find naught but vexation and vanity in the reign of the Sixteenth Louis? Subtle variation may be had by substituting as foundation, *sauce à la régence* or *sauce à la princesse* for *sauce Béchamel;* while a sensation apart springs from the lofty alliance between oysters and mushrooms.

How natural that for masterpieces in mushrooms royalty so often has stood sponsor! Upon the Prince of Wurtemberg rests the glorious responsibility of Seine shad *à la purée de champignons*. If history records not his name, a prince —in spirit at least—must also have been the first happy man to eat red mullets *aux champignons*, or eels *aux huîtres et aux champignons;* show yourself as princely before you are a week older. While a king was he who first smiled upon that kingly *ragoût* of mushrooms, mussels, and shrimps. Be you a king in your turn—there are few pleasures equal to it

"For white fowls of all sort," Mrs Glasse recommends her mushroom sauce, thus giving loose reins to the artist's fancy. The fowl may be boiled, and then rich with cream must be the sauce that redeems it from insipidity. It may be roasted, and then let the mushrooms be somewhat more in evidence. Or it may be broiled, and then mayhap it would be wise to grill the mushrooms whole, instead of converting them into sauce. Or—here is another suggestion, and be thankful for it—mince your chicken, which toast will receive gladly as a covering and set upon it, as already upon *œufs brouillés*, the mushrooms grilled in butter Long might you live, far might you wander, before chancing upon another delicacy so worthy. Though, truth to tell—and where gastronomy is the subject it is always best to be honest—*croquettes de poulet aux champignons* seem well-nigh worthier. If you would decide for yourself, try both, and joy go with you in the trying.

An afterthought: dress livers with mushroom sauce, and this is the manner in which it should be done. "Take some pickled or fresh mushrooms, cut small—both if you have them—and let the livers be bruised fine, with a good deal of parsley chopped small, a spoonful or two of catchup, a glass of white wine, and as much good gravy as will make sauce enough; thicken it with a piece of butter rolled in flour. This does for either roast or boiled."

For the rest, how count the innumerable

ways in which the mushroom adds to the gaiety of the gourmand? What would the *vol-au-vent* be without it? What the "Fine Pye," made otherwise of carps and artichokes and crayfishes' feet and lobster claws and nutmeg and cloves alone? What, according to the "Complete Court Cook," so proper for the second course as the patty all of mushrooms? What garniture fairer for "ragoo" or *fricassée*, according to the same authority, than mushroom *farcis*? But, however they may be served and eaten, mushrooms you must make yours at any cost. To say that you do not like them is confession of your own philistinism. Learn to like them; *will* to like them, or else your sojourn on this earth will be a wretched waste. You will have lived your life in vain if, at its close, you have missed one of its finest emotions.

THE INCOMPARABLE ONION

Too often the poet sees but the tears that live in an onion; not the smiles. And yet the smiles are there, broad and genial, or subtle and tender. "Rose among roots," its very name revives memories of pleasant feasting; its fragrance is rich forecast of delights to come. Without it, there would be no gastronomic art. Banish it from the kitchen, and all pleasure of eating flies with it. Its presence lends colour and enchantment to the most modest dish; its absence reduces the rarest dainty to hopeless insipidity, and the diner to despair.

The secret of good cooking lies in the discreet and sympathetic treatment of the onion. For what culinary masterpiece is there that may not be improved by it? It gives vivacity to soup, life to sauce; it is the "poetic soul" of the salad bowl; the touch of romance in the well-cooked vegetable. To it, sturdiest joint and lightest stew, crisp rissole and stimulating stuffing look for inspiration and charm—and never are they disappointed! But woe betide the unwary woman who would approach it for sacrilegious ends. If life holds nothing better than the onion in the right hand, it offers nothing sadder and more degrading than the onion brutalised. Wide is the gulf fixed between the delicate sauce of a Prince de Soubise, and the coarse, unsavoury sausage and onion mess of the Strand. Let the perfection of the first be your ideal; the horrid coarseness of the latter shun as you would the devil.

The fragrance of this "wine-scented" esculent not only whets the appetite; it abounds in associations glad and picturesque. All Italy is in the fine, penetrating smell; and all Provence; and all Spain. An onion or garlic-scented atmosphere hovers alike over the narrow *calli* of Venice, the cool courts of Cordova, and the thronged amphitheatre of Arles. It is only the atmosphere breathed by the Latin peoples of the South, so that ever must it suggest blue skies and endless sunshine, cypress groves and olive orchards. For the traveller it is interwoven with memories of the golden canvases of Titian, the song of Dante, the music of Mascagni. The violet may not work a sweeter spell, nor the carnation yield a more intoxicating perfume.

And some men there have been in the past to rank the onion as a root sacred to Aphrodite, food for lovers. To the poetry of it none but the dull and brutal can long remain indifferent.

Needless, then, to dwell upon its more prosaic side: upon its power as a tonic, its value as a medicine. Medicinal properties it has, as the drunkard knows full well. But why consider the drunkard? Leave him to the tender mercies of the doctor. *Gourmandise*, or the love of good eating, here the one and only concern, is opposed to excess. "Every man who eats to indigestion, or makes himself drunk, runs the risk of being erased from the list of its votaries."

The onion is but the name for a large family, of which shallots, garlic, and chives are chief and most honoured varieties. Moreover, country and climate work upon it changes many and strange. In the south it beomes larger and more opulent, like the women. And yet, as it increases in size, it loses in strength—who shall say why? And the loss truly is an improvement Our own onion often is strong even unto rankness. Therefore, as all good housewives understand, the Spanish species for most purposes may be used instead, and great will be the gain thereby. Still further south, still further east, you will journey but to find the onion fainter in flavour, until in India it seems but a pale parody of its English prototype. And again, at different seasons, very different are its most salient qualities. In great gladness of heart everyone must look forward to the dainy little spring onion: adorable as vegetable cooked in good white sauce, inscrutable as guardian spirit of fresh green salad, irreproachable as pickle in vinegar and mustard

Garlic is one of the most gracious gifts of the gods to men—a gift, alas! too frequently abused. In the vegetable world, it has something of the value of scarlet among colours, of the clarionet's call in music. Brazen, and crude, and screaming, when dragged into undue prominence, it may yet be made to harmonise divinely with fish and fowl, with meat, and other greens. Thrown wholesale into a salad, it is odious and insupportable; but used to rub the salad bowl, and then cast aside, its virtue may not be exaggerated. For it, as for lovers, the season of seasons is the happy spring time. Its true home is Provence. What would be the land of the troubadour and the Félibre without the *ail* that festoons every greengrocer's shop, that adorns every dish at every banquet of rich and poor alike? As well rid *bouillabaisse* of its saffron as of its *ail;* as well forget the *pomme d'amour* in the sauce for *macaroni*, or the rosemary and the thyme on the spit with the little birds. The verse of Roumanille and Mistral smells sweet of *ail;* Tartarin and Numa Roumestan are heroes nourished upon it. It is the very essence of *farandoles* and *ferrades*, of bull-fights and water tournaments. A pinch of *ail*, a *coup de vin*, and then—

> Viva la joia,
> Fidon la tristessa!

And all the while we, in the cold, gloomy north, eat garlic and are hated for it by friends and foes. Only in the hot south can life *ail*-inspired pass for a *galejado* or jest.

To the onion, the shallot is as the sketch to the finished picture; slighter, it may be; but often subtler and more suggestive. Unrivalled in salads and sauces, it is without compare in the sumptuous seasoning of the most fantastic viands It does not assert itself with the fury and pertinacity of garlic; it does not announce its presence with the self-consciousness of the onion. It appeals by more refined devices, by gentler means, and is to be prized accordingly. Small and brown, it is pleasant to look upon as the humble wild rose by the side of the *Gloire de Dijon* And, though it never attain to the untempered voluptuousness of the onion, it develops its sweetness and strength under the hottest suns of summer: in July, August, and September, does it mature; then do its charms ripen; then may it be enjoyed in full perfection, and satisfy the most riotous gluttony.

Shallots for summer by preference, but chives for spring: the delicate chives, the long, slim leaves, fair to look upon, sweet to smell, sweeter still to eat in crisp green salad. The name is a little poem; the thing itself falls not far short of the divine. Other varieties there be, other offshoots of the great onion—mother of all; none, however, of greater repute, of wider possibilities than these. To know them well is to master the fundamental principles of the art of cookery. But this is knowledge given unto the few; the many, no doubt, will remain for ever in the outer darkness, where the onion is condemned to everlasting companionship with the sausage—not altogether their fault, perhaps. In cookery, as in all else, too often the blind do lead the blind. But a few years since and a "delicate diner," an authority unto himself at least, produced upon the art of dining a book, not without reputation. But to turn to its index is to find not one reference to the onion. all the poetry gone; little but prose left! And this from an authority!

The onion, as a dish, is excellent; as seasoning it has still more pleasant and commodious merits. The modern *chef* uses it chiefly to season; the ancient *cordon bleu* set his wits to work to discover spices and aromatic ingredients wherewith to season it Thus, according to Philemon,—

> If you want an onion, just consider
> What great expense it takes to make it good;
> You must have cheese, and honey, and sesame,
> Oil, leeks, and vinegar, and assafœtida,
> To dress it up with; for by itself the onion
> Is bitter and unpleasant to the taste.

A pretty mess, indeed; and who is there brave enough to-day to test it? Honey and onion! it suggests the ingenious contrivances of the mediæval kitchen. The most daring experiment now would be a dash of wine, red or white, a suspicion of mustard, a touch of tomato in the sauce for onions, stewed or boiled, baked or stuffed. To venture upon further flights of fancy the average cook would consider indiscreet, though to the genius all things are possible. However, its talents for giving savour and character to other dishes is inexhaustible.

There is no desire more natural than that of knowledge; there is no knowledge nobler than that of the "gullet-science." "The discovery of a new dish does more for the happiness of the human race than the discovery of a planet!" What would be Talleyrand's record but for that moment of inspiration when, into the mysteries of Parmesan with soup, he initiated his countrymen? To what purpose the Crusades, had Crusaders not seen and and loved the garlic on the plains of Askalon, and brought it home with them, their one glorious trophy. To a pudding Richelieu gave his name; the Prince de Soubise lent his to a sauce, and thereby won for it immortality.

A benefactor to his race indeed he was: worthy of a shrine in the Temple of Humanity. For, plucking the soul from the onion, he laid bare its hidden and sweetest treasure to the elect. Scarce a sauce is served that owes not fragrance and flavour to the wine-scented root; to it, *Béarnaise*, *Maître d'Hôtel*, *Espagnole*, *Italienne*, *Béchamel*, *Provençale*, and who shall say how many more? look for the last supreme touch that redeems them from insipid commonplace. But *Sauce Soubise* is the very idealisation of the onion, its very essence; at once delicate and strong; at once as simple and as perfect as all great works of art.

The plodding painter looks upon a nocturne by Whistler, and thinks how easy, how preposterously easy! A touch here, a stroke there, and the thing is done But let him try! And so with *Sauce Soubise*. Turn to the first cookery book at hand, and read the *recipe*. "Peel four large onions and cut them into thin slices; sprinkle a little pepper and salt upon them, together with a small quantity of nutmeg; put them into a saucepan with a slice of fresh butter, and steam gently"—let them smile, the true artist would say—"till they are soft." But why go on with elaborate directions? Why describe the exact quantity of flour, the size of the potato, the proportions of milk and cream to be added? Why explain in detail the process of rubbing through a sieve? In telling or the reading these matters seem not above the intelligence of a little child But in the actual making, only the artist understands the secret of perfection, and his understanding is born within him, not borrowed from dry statistics and formal tables. He may safely be left to vary his methods; he may add sugar, he may omit nutmeg; he may fry the onions instead of boiling, for love of the tinge of brown, rich and sombre, thus obtained. But, whatever he does, always with a wooden spoon will he stir his savoury mixture; always, as result, produce a godlike sauce which the mutton cutlets of Paradise, vying with Heine's roast goose, will offer of their own accord at celestial banquets. What wonder that a certain famous French count despised the prosaic politician who had never heard of cutlets *à la Soubise?*

However, not alone in sauce can the condescending onion come to the aid of dull, substantial flesh and fowl. Its virtue, when joined to sage in stuffing, who will gainsay? Even chestnuts, destined to stuff to repletion the yawning turkey, cannot afford to ignore the insinuating shallot or bolder garlic; while no meat comes into the market that will not prove the better and the sweeter for at least a suspicion of onion or of *ail*. A barbarian truly is the cook who flings a mass of fried onions upon the tender steak, and then thinks to offer you a rare and dainty dish. Not with such wholesale brutality can the ideal be attained. The French chef has more tact. He will take his *gigot* and sympathetically prick it here and there with garlic or with chives, even as it is roasting; and whoever has never tasted mutton thus prepared knows not the sublimest heights of human happiness. Or else he will make a *bouquet garni* of his own, entirely of these aromatic roots and leaves, and fasten it in dainty fashion to the joint; pleasure is doubled when he forgets to remove it, and the meat is placed upon the table, still bearing its delicious decoration. Moods there be that call for stronger effects: moods when the blazing poppy field of a Monet pleases more than the quiet moonlight of a Cazin; when Tennyson is put aside for Swinburne. At such times, call for a shoulder of mutton, well stuffed with onions, and still further satiate your keen, vigorous appetite with a bottle of Beaune or Pomard. But here, a warning: eat and drink with at least a pretence of moderation. Remember that, but for an excess of shoulder of mutton and onions, Napoleon might not have been defeated at Leipzig.

But at all times, and in all places, onions clamour for moderation. A salad of tomatoes buried under thick layers of this powerful esculent must disgust; gently sprinkled with chopped-up chives or shallots, it enraptures. Potatoes *à la Lyonnaise*, curried eggs, Irish stew,

Guiyas, *ragoût*, alike demand restraint in their preparation, a sweet reasonableness in the hand that distributes the onion.

For the delicate diner, as for the drunkard, onion soup has charm. It is of the nature of *sauce Soubise*, and what mightier recommendation could be given it? Thus Dumas, the high priest of the kitchen, made it: a dozen onions—Spanish by preference—minced with discretion, fried in freshest of fresh butter until turned to a fair golden yellow, he boiled in three pints or so of water, adequately seasoned with salt and pepper; and then, at the end of twenty full minutes, he mixed with this preparation the yolks of two or three eggs, and poured the exquisite liquid upon bread, cut and ready. At the thought alone the mouth waters, the eye brightens. The adventurous, now and again, add ham or rice, vegetables or a *bouquet garni*. But this as you will, according to the passing hour's leisure. Only of one thing make sure—in Dumas confidence is ever to be placed without doubt or hesitation.

Dumas' soup for dinner; but for breakfast the unrivalled omelette of Brillat-Savarin. It is made after this fashion: the roes of two carp, a piece of fresh tunny, and shallots, well hashed and mixed, are thrown into a saucepan with a lump of butter beyond reproach, and whipped up till the butter is melted, which, says the great one, "constitutes the speciality of the omelette;" in the meantime, let some one prepare, upon an oval dish, a mixture of butter and parsley, lemon juice, and chives—not shallots here, let the careless note—the plate to be left waiting over hot embers; next beat up twelve eggs, pour in the roes and tunny, stir with the zeal and sympathy of an artist, spread upon the plate that waits so patiently, serve at once; and words fail to describe the ecstasy that follows. Especially, to quote again so eminent an authority, let the omelette "be washed down with some good old wine, and you will see wonders," undreamed of by haschish or opium eater.

When the little delicate spring onion is smelt in the land, a shame, indeed, it would be to waste its tender virginal freshness upon sauce and soup. Rather refrain from touching it with sharp knife or cruel chopper, but in its graceful maiden form boil it, smother it in rich pure cream, and serve it on toast, to the unspeakable delectation of the devout. Life yields few more precious moments. Until spring comes, however, you may do worse than apply the same treatment to the older onion. In this case, as pleasure's crown of pleasure, adorn the surface with grated Gruyère, and, like the ancient hero, you will wish your throat as long as a crane's neck, that so you might the longer and more leisurely taste what you swallow.

Onions *farcis* are beloved by the epicure. A nobler dish could scarce be devised. You may make your forcemeats of what you will, beef or mutton, fowl or game; you may, an' you please, add truffles, mushrooms, olives, and capers. But know one thing; tasteless it will prove, and lifeless, unless bacon lurk unseen somewhere within its depths. Ham will answer in a way, but never so well as humbler bacon. The onion that lends itself most kindly to this device is the Spanish.

One word more. As the *ite missa est* of the discourse let this truth—a blessing in itself—be spoken. As with meat, so with vegetables, few are not the better for the friendly companionship of the onion, or one of its many offshoots. Peas, beans, tomatoes, egg-plant are not indifferent to its blandishments. If honour be paid to the first pig that uprooted a truffle, what of the first man who boiled an onion? And what of the still mightier genius who first used it as seasoning for his daily fare? Every *gourmet* should rise up and call him blessed.

THE TRIUMPHANT TOMATO

THE triumph of the tomato has given hungry men and women a new lease of pleasure Sad and drear were the days when the *gourmet* thought to feast, and the beautiful scarlet fruit had no place upon his table. The ancient *chef* knew it not, nor the mediæval artist who, even without it, could create marvellous works the modern may not hope to rival. Like so many good things, it first saw the light in that happy Western Continent where the canvas-back duck makes its home and shad swim in fertile rivers. What, indeed, was life, what the gift of eating, before the Columbus of the kitchen had discovered the tomato, the turkey, and the yellow Indian corn? Reflect upon it, and be grateful that you, at least, were not born in the Dark Age of cookery!

Poor, stupid man! a treasure was presented to him freely and generously, and he thrust it from him The tomato offered itself a willing sacrifice, and he scorned it, mistaking gold for dross. The American—and long years in purgatory will not redeem his fault—looked upon it with suspicion. To-day, it is true, he honours it aright: in the summer-time he bows down before its gay freshness; in the winter he cherishes it in tins. It has become as indispensable to him as salt or butter. He values it at its true worth. But still, half a century has not passed since he doubted it, heaping insults upon its trusting sweetness. He fancied poison lurked within it. O the cruel fancy! There it was, perfect and most desirable, and he, blind fool, would not touch it until endless hours of stewing had lessened, if not utterly destroyed, its fresh young charms. And the Englishman was no wiser. Within the last decade only has he welcomed the stranger at his gates, and at the best his welcome has been but halting and half-hearted. The many continue obstinately to despise it; the few have pledged their allegiance with reservations. The Latin, and even the wild Hun, were converted without a fear of misgiving while the Anglo-Saxon faltered and was weak. Many and beautiful are the strange dishes the tomato adorns in Magyarland. Was there ever a *menu* in sunny Italy that did not include this meat or that vegetable *al pomodoro?* The very Spaniard, whom rumour weds irrevocably to garlic, nourishes a tender passion for the voluptuous red fruit, and wins rapture from it. And deep and true is the Provençal's love for his *pomme d'amour;* is not the name a measure of his affection? The Love Apple! Were there, after all, tomatoes in Judea, and were these the apples that comforted the love-sick Shulamite?

Now that the tomato has forced universal recognition; now that in England it lends glory of colour to the greengrocer's display; now that the hothouse defeats the cruel siege of the seasons, and mild May, as well as mellow September, yields apples of love, pause a moment, turn from the trivial cares of life, to meditate upon its manifold virtues.

The tomato as a vegetable should be the first point of the meditation. Let us reflect. Stewed, though not as in America of old, until all flavour is lost, it has the merit of simplicity by no means to be underestimated: drained of the greater part of its juice, thickened slightly with flour, it cannot disappoint. *Au gratin*, it aspires to more delirious joys: the pleasure yielded develops in proportion to the pains taken to produce it. Into a baking dish olive oil is poured in moderation; a sprinkling of salt and pepper and fragrant herbs well powdered, together with bread-crumbs duly grated, follows; next the tomatoes, eager and blushing, whole or in dainty halves, as the impulse of the moment may prompt; more breadcrumbs and pepper and salt and herbs must cover them gently, more oil be poured upon the stirring harmony; and an hour in the oven will turn you out as pretty a side-dish as was ever devised by ingenious Mrs Glasse, who—O the pity of it—lived too soon for fond dalliance with love's crowning vegetable.

Farcies tomatoes may not easily be surpassed. Upon your whim or choice it will depend whether you stuff them whole, or cut them in half for so ineffable a purpose. And upon your whim likewise depends the special forcemeat used. Chopped mushrooms, parsley and shallot, seasoned with discretion, leave little to ask for. Prepare, instead, sausage meat, garlic, parsley, tarragon, and chives, and the tomatoes so stuffed you may without pedantry call *à la Grimod de la Reynière* But whatever you call them, count upon happiness in the eating.

Second point of the meditation: the tomato as an auxiliary If you have learned the trick of association, at once you see before you a steaming harmony in pale yellow and scarlet, the long soft tubes of *macaroni* or *spaghetti* encompassed round about by a deep stream of tomatoes stewed and seasoned; at once you feast upon *macaroni al pomodoro* and Chianti, and Italy lies, like a map, before your mind's eye, its towns and villages marked by this dish of dishes. With rice, tomatoes are no less in pleasant, peaceful unity; in stuffed *paprika*, or pepper, they find their true affinity. Grilled, they make a sympathetic garniture for *filet piqué à la Richelieu;* stuffed, they are the proper accompaniment of *tournedos à la Leslie;* neatly halved, they serve as a foundation to soles *à la Loie Fuller.* Chickens clamour for them as ally, and so does the saltest of salt cod. In a word, a new combination they might with ease provide for every day in the year. Enough will have been said if this one truth is established: there is scarce a fish or fowl, scarce any meat or vegetable, that is not the better and the nobler for the temporary union with the tomato.

And now, the third point of the meditation, which, too often, escapes the prosaic, unmeditative islander: the tomato as a dish for breakfast. Only recently it was thus that two of rare beauty and sweet savour fulfilled their destiny: on a plate fasioned by barbarous potters on the banks of the Danube, where the love-apple grows in gay profusion, stretched a thin, crisp slice of bacon decoratively streaked with fat and grilled to a turn; it bore, as twin flowers, the two tomatoes, also grilled, fragrant, tender, delectable. Surely here was a poetic prelude to the day's toil. To Belgium all praise be given for teaching that, stewed and encircling buttered or scrambled eggs, tomatoes may again enliven the breakfast table, that bitter test of conjugal devotion; to France, the credit of spreading them at the bottom of plate or dish as a bed for eggs artistically poached or fried. History records the names of generals

The Triumphant Tomato

and dates of battles, but what chronicler has immortalised the genius who first enclosed tomatoes in an omelet? This is a brutal, ungrateful world we live in.

And now pass on to the fourth heading, and new ecstasies: the tomato as salad. Remember that the tomatoes must be deftly sliced in their skins or else the juice escapes; that a touch of onion or garlic is indispensable; that the dressing must be of oil and vinegar, pepper and salt; unless, of course, a *mayonnaise* be made. Another weird salad there is with qualities to endear it to the morbid and neurotic. Let it be explained briefly, that lurid description may not be thought to exaggerate lurid attraction: drop your tomatoes, brilliantly red as the abhorred Scarlet Woman, into hot water in order to free them of their skins; place them whole, and in passionate proximity, in a dish of silver or delicate porcelain; smother them under a thick layer of whipped cream. For the sake of decoration and the unexpected, stick in here and there a pistachio nut, and thank the gods for the new sensation.

In soup, thin or clear, the tomato knows no

rival; in sauce, it stands supreme, ranking worthily with the four classical sauces of the French *cuisine*. And here, a suggestion to be received with loud, jubilant *Alleluias!* Follow the example of Attila's heirs, and, as last touch, pour cream upon your tomato sauce. He who has known and eaten and loved *paprika gefüllte* in the wilds of Transylvania, will bear willing witness to the admirable nature of this expedient.

The more devout, the professed worshipper, will eat his love-apple without artificial device of cookery or dressing, with only salt for savour. For this excess of devotion, however, unqualified commendation would not be just. Unadorned the tomato is not adorned the most.

But cook or serve it as you will, see that it be eaten by you and yours—that is the main thing. The tomatoes that make glad the heart of the loiterer in Covent Garden are fresh as the sweet breath of May.

A DISH OF SUNSHINE

"The weather is regarded as the very nadir and scoff of conversational topics." How can the ingenious housewife talk of aught else in the Winter season? Not because, as Mr Stevenson argues, "the dramatic element in scenery is far more tractable in language, and far more human both in import and suggestion, than the stable features of the landscape," but because upon it she is dependent for ease and success in making her every luncheon and dinner a culinary triumph.

Of what avail the morning's conference with the greengrocer's boy, or even the conscientious visit to the greengrocer's shop or the ramble through the market—unless, perhaps, and happily, her pockets be lined with gold, when hothouse vegetables, and out-of-season delicacies, must be paid for with the alacrity of a Crœsus? Otherwise, dark, hopeless despair seizes upon her? Must she not brood in abject melancholy when the hideous truth is revealed to her that earth's resources are limited to turnip-tops and Brussels sprouts, with, it may be, a few Jerusalem artichokes thrown in? Celery, the lordly, is frozen. Cauliflower, the fragrant, frost-bitten irretrievably, will not yield to the most urgent inducements of hot water. Lettuce is a thing of the past and of the future. Sad and drear indeed is the immediate prospect. For surely turnip-tops are a delusion, and against the monotony of sprouts the aspiring soul rebels.

It is at this crisis that hope flames right in a strangely neglected corner. Italian sunshine and blue skies, concentrated in flour paste, wrought into tubes and ribbons, squares and lozenges, come to gladden the sinking heart and cheer the drooping spirits. Why despair when *macaroni* is always to be had, inestimable as a vegetable, unrivalled as an *entrée*, a perfect meal, if you choose, in itself?

Upon the imagination of those to whom food is something besides a mere satisfaction to carnal appetite, *macaroni* works a strange, subtle spell. The very name conjures up sweet poetic visions; it is the magic crystal or beryl stone, in which may be seen known things, dear to the memory: smiling valleys where the vines are festooned, not as Virgil saw them, from elm to elm, but from mulberry to mulberry; and where the beautiful, broad-horned, white oxen drag, in solemn dignity, the crawling plough; olive-clad slopes and lonely stone palms; the gleam of sunlit rivers winding with the reeds and the tall, slim poplars; the friendly wayside *trattoria* and the pleasant refrain of the beaming *cameriere*, "*Subito Signora; ecco!*"—a refrain ceaseless as the buzzing of bees among the clover. In a dish of *macaroni* lies all Italy for the woman with eyes to see or a heart to feel.

Or visions more personal, more intimate, she may summon for her own delight; the midday halt and lunch in Castiglione del Lago on its gentle hill-top, the blue of Thrasymene's lake shining between the olives, and all fair to behold, save the *padrone* with his conscienceless charges for the bowl of *macaroni* that had been so good in the eating. Or else, perhaps, the evening meal in the long refectory at Monte

Oliveto, with the white-robed brothers; or, again, the unforgetable breakfast at Pompeii's *Albergo del Sole*, the good wine ranged upon the old tree trunk that serves as central column, the peacock, tail outspread, strutting about among the chairs and tables, the overpowering sweetness of the flowering bean stealing, from near fields, through open doors and windows. Or, still again, the thought of Pompeii sends one off upon the journey from its ruined streets to Naples—on one side the Bay, on the other the uninterrupted line of villages, every low white house adorned with garlands of *macaroni* drying peacefully and swiftly in the hot sun. And a few pence only will it cost to dream such dreams of beauty and of gladness.

Many as are the devices for preparing this stuff that dreams are made of, none can excel the simplest of all. Eat it the way the Italian loves it, and for yourself you open up new vistas of pleasure. And what could be easier? In water well salted—upon the salt much depends—the *macaroni*, preferably in the large generous tubes, is boiled for twenty minutes, or half an hour, until it is as soft as soft may

A Dish of Sunshine

be without breaking. A capacious bowl, its sides well buttered and sprinkled with grated Parmesan cheese, must wait in readiness. Into it put the *macaroni*, well drained of the water, into its midst drop a large piece of sweet, fresh butter, and sprinkle, without stint, more of the indispensable Parmesan; mix wisely and with discrimination; and then eat to your soul's, or stomach's, content. To further your joy, have at your side a flash of Chianti, pure and strong, standing in no need of baptism. The gods never fared better. But, one word of advice: if this dish you serve for luncheon, defy convention, and make it the first and last and only course. It may seem meagre in the telling. But to treat it with due respect and justice much must be eaten, and this much makes more impossible even to the hopeful.

Another word of advice: never break or cut the *macaroni* into small pieces; the cook who dares to disobey in this particular deserves instant and peremptory dismissal. Where is the poetry, where the art, if it can be eaten with as little trouble and planning as an everyday potato, or a mess of greens? Who, that has seen, can forget the skilful Italian winding the long steaming tubes around and around his fork, his whole soul and intelligence concentrated upon the pretty feat of transposing these tubes from his fork to his mouth. It is difficult; yes, especially for the foreigner; but where is the pleasure without pain? As well tear your Troyon or your Diaz into shreds, and enjoy it in bits, as violate the virginal lengths of your *macaroni*.

In more lavish mood, prepare it *al sugo*, and no cause need you fear for regret. It is wellnigh as simple; the *macaroni*, or better still *spaghetti*, the smaller, daintier variety, once boiled, is taken from the water only to be plunged in rich gravy, its quantity varying according to the quantity of *spaghetti* used; let it boil anew, or rather simmer, until each long tube is well saturated; then, add the cheese and butter, and say your *Benedicite* with a full heart.

Or, would you have it richer still, and so tempt Providence? Make tomato the foundation of the gravy, spice it with cloves, bring

A Dish of Sunshine

out the sweet *bouquet garni*, serve with butter and Parmesan cheese as before, and call the result *Macaroni à la Napolitaine*. *Spaghetti*, here again, will answer the purpose as well, nor will the pretty, flat, wavy ribbon species come amiss. To court perfection, rely upon mushrooms for one of the chief elements in this adorable concoction, and the whole world over you may travel without finding a dish worthy to compete with it. *Macaroni* can yield nothing more exquisite, though not yet are its resources exhausted.

Au gratin it is also to be commended. The preliminary boiling may now, as always, be taken for granted. With its chosen and well-tried accompaniments of butter and Parmesan cheese, and steeped in a good white sauce, it may simmer gently over the fire until the sympathetic butter be absorbed; then in a decently prepared dish, and covered with bread-crumbs, it should bake until it is warmed into a golden-brown harmony that enraptures the eye. Or with stronger seasoning, with onion and pepper and cayenne, you may create a savoury beyond compare. Or combined with the same ingredients you may stew your *macaroni* in milk, and revel in *macaroni sauté*; worse a hundred times, truly, might you fare.

But, if you would be wholly reckless, why, then try *Macaroni à la Pontife*, and know that human ambition may scarce pretend to nobler achievements. For a mould of goodly proportions you fill with *macaroni* and forcemeat of fowl and larks and bits of bacon and mushrooms and game filleted; and this ineffable arrangement you moisten with gravy and allow to simmer slowly, as befits its importance, for an hour; eat it, and at last you too, with Faust, may hail the fleeting moment, and bid it stay, because it is so fair!

In puddings and pies *macaroni* is most excellent. But if you be not lost beyond redemption, never sweeten either one or the other; the suggestion of such sacrilege alone is horrid. Into little croquettes it may by cunning hands be modelled; *en timbale*, in well-shaped mould, it reveals new and welcome possibilities. With fish it assimilates admirably; in soup it is above criticism. It will strengthen the flavour of chestnuts, nor will it disdain the stimulating influence of wine, white or red. And in the guise of *nouilles*, or nudels, it may be stuffed with forcemeat of fowl or beef, and so clamour for the rich tomato sauce.

ON SALADS

To speak of salads in aught but the most reverential spirit were sacrilege. To be honoured aright, they should be eaten only in the company of the devout or in complete solitude—and perhaps this latter is the wiser plan. Who, but the outer barbarian, will not with a good salad,

> A book, a taper, and a cup
> Of country wine, divinely sup?

Over your hot meats you cannot linger; if alone with them, and read you must, a common newspaper, opened at the day's despatches, best serves your purpose; else, your gravies and sauces congeal into a horrid white mess upon your plate, and tepid is every unsavoury morsel your fork carries to your mouth. But over any one of the "salad clan"—lettuce or tomato, beans or potato, as fancy prompts—you can revel at leisure in your Balzac, your Heine, your Montaigne, which, surely, it would be desecration to spread open by the side of the steaming roast or the prosaic bacon and eggs. There has always seemed one thing lacking in Omar's Paradise: a salad, he should have bargained for with his Book of Verses, his Jug of Wine, and Loaf of Bread "underneath the Bough."

Far behind has the Continent left Great Britain in the matter of salads. To eat them in perfection you must cross the Channel—as, indeed, you must in the pursuit of all the daintiest dishes—and travel still farther than France. The French will give you for breakfast a bowl of *Soissons*, for dinner a *Romaine*, which long survive as tender memories; even the humble dandelion they have enlisted in the good cause. With the Italian you will fare no less well; better it may be, for, with the poetic feeling that has disappeared for ever from their art and architecture, they fill the salad bowl at times with such delicate conceits as tender young violet leaves, so that you may smell the spring in the blossoms at your throat, while you devour it in the greens set before you. But in

Germany, though there may be less play of fancy in the choice of materials, there is far greater poetry in the mixing of them. As an atonement for that offence against civilisation, the midday dinner, the Germans have invented a late supper that defies the critic: the very meanest *Speise-Saal* is transfigured when the gaslight falls softly on the delicious potato or cucumber or herring salads of the country, flanked by the tall slim glasses of amber Rhenish wine But, excelling Germany, even as Germany excels France, Hungary is the true home of the salad. It would take a book to exhaust the praise it there inspires. To die eating salad on the banks of the Danube to the wail of the Czardas—that would be the true death! What, however, save the ideals realised, is to be effected in a land where tomatoes are as plentiful as are potatoes in Ireland?

The Briton, it must be admitted, has of late progressed. Gone is the time when his favourite salad was a horror unspeakable: an onion and a lettuce served whole, chopped up by himself, smothered in salt and pepper, and fairly sluiced with vinegar. To understand the full iniquity of it, you must remember what an excess of vinegar the stalwart Briton was equal to in those days, now happily past. An imperial pint, Mr Weller's friend, the coachman with the hoarse voice, took with his oysters without betraying the least emotion. As benighted, smacking no less of the Dark Ages, is the custom of serving with cheese a lettuce (of the long crisp species known as *cos* in the cookery books), cut ruthlessly in halves. You are supposed to dip the leaves into salt, and afterwards return thanks with a grateful heart. Many there are who will still eat lettuce in this fashion with their tea; the curious student of evolution can point to it as a survival of the old barbarism; to the mustard and cress or cucumber sandwiches which have replaced it, as a higher phase of development

But, though these sorry customs still survive here and there, even as superstitions linger among ignorant peasants, British eyes are opening to the truth. The coming of the salad in England marks the passing of the Englishman from barbarous depth to civilised heights. Has he not exchanged his old-love Frith for Whistler, and has he not risen from G. P. R. James to George Meredith? Not a whit less important in the history of his civilisation is his emancipation from that vile, vinegar-drenched abomination to the succulent tomato, the unrivalled potato, well "fatigued" in the "capacious salad-bowl."

Of every woman worthy of the name, it is the duty to master the secret of the perfect salad, and to prepare it for her own—and man's—greater comfort and joy in this life, and—who knows?—salvation in the next. This secret is all in the dressing. It is easy enough to buy in the market, or order at the greengrocer's a lettuce, or a cucumber, or a pound of tomatoes. But to make of them a masterpiece, there's the rub. Upon the dressing and "fatiguing" success depends. The mission of the lettuce, the resources of the bean were undreamed of until the first woman—it must have been a woman!—divined the virtue that lies in the harmonious combination of oil and vinegar. Vinegar alone and undiluted is for the vulgar; mixed with oil it as much surpasses nectar and ambrosia as these hitherto have been reckoned superior to the liquors of mere human brewing. Of *mayonnaise* nothing need as yet be said; it ranks rather with sauces, irreproachable when poured upon salmon, or chicken, or lobster—upon the simpler and more delicate salads it seems wellnigh too strong and coarse. The one legitimate dressing in these cases is made of vinegar and oil, pepper and salt, and, on certain rare occasions, mustard.

As with sauces, it is simple to put down in black and white the several ingredients of the good dressing. But what of the proportions? What of the methods of mixing? In the large towns of the United States where men and women delight in the pleasures of the table, are specialists who spend their afternoons going from house to house, preparing the salads for the day's coming great event. And perhaps, in the end, all mankind may see advantages in this division of labour. For only the genius born can mix a salad dressing as it should be mixed. Quantities of pepper and salt, of oil and vinegar for him (or her) are not measured by rule or recipe, but by inspiration. You may generalise and insist upon one spoonful of oil for every guest and one for the bowl—somewhat in the manner of tea-making—and then one-third the quantity of vinegar. But out of these proportions the Philistine will evolve for you a nauseating concoction; the initiated, a dressing of transcendental merit

As much depends upon the mixing as upon the proportions. The foolish pour in first their oil, then their vinegar, and leave the rest to chance, with results one shudders to remember. The two must be mixed together even as they are poured over the salad, and here the task but begins. For next, they must be mixed with the salad. To "fatigue" it the French call this special part of the process, and indeed, to create a work of art, you must mix and mix and mix until you are fatigued yourself, and your tomatoes or potatoes reduced to one-half their original bulk. Then will the dressing have soaked through and through them, then will every mouthful be a special plea for gluttony, an eloquent argument for the one vice that need not pall with years.

One other ingredient must not be omitted

here, since it is as essential as the oil itself. This is the onion—

> Rose among roots, the maiden fair,
> Wine-scented and poetic soul

of every salad. You may rub with it the bowl, you may chop it up fine and sprinkle with it the lettuce, as you might sprinkle an omelet with herbs. But there, in one form or another, it must be. The French have a tendency to abuse it; they will cut it in great slices to spread between layers of tomatoes or cucumbers. But there is a touch of grossness in this device. It is just the *soupçon* you crave, just the subtle flavour it alone can impart. You do not want your salad, when it comes on the table, to suggest nothing so much as the stewed steak and onions shops in the Strand! The fates forbid.

"What diversities soever there be in herbs, all are shuffled up together under the name of sallade." And Montaigne wrote in sadness, knowing well that there could be no error more fatal. Have you ever asked for a salad at the greengrocer's, and been offered a collection of weeds befitting nothing so much as Betsy Prig's capacious pocket? Have you ever, at the table of the indifferent, been served with the same collection plentifully drenched with "salad cream"? But these are painful memories, speedily to be put aside and banished for evermore. Some combinations there are of herbs or greens or vegetables unspeakably delicious, even in the thought thereof. But it is not at haphazard, by an unsympathetic greengrocer, they can be made; not in haste, from bottles of atrocities, they can be dressed. They are the result of conscientious study, of consummate art.

Besides, some varieties there be of flavour too delicate to be tampered with: for instance, the cabbage lettuce, as the vulgar call it, which comes in about Easter time, but which, at the cost of a little trouble, can be had all the year round. For some reason unknown, your hardhearted greengrocer, half the time, objects to it seriously, declares it not to be found from end to end of Covent Garden. But let him understand that upon his providing it depends your custom, and he fetches it—the unprincipled one—fast enough. The ragged outer leaves pulled away, crisp and fresh is the heart, a cool green and white harmony not to be touched by brutal knife. The leaves must be torn apart, gently and lovingly, as the painter plays with the colours on his palette. Then, thrown into the bowl which already has been well rubbed with onion, and slices of hard-boiled egg laid upon the top for adornment and flavouring alike, at once may the dressing of oil and vinegar and salt and pepper be poured on, and the process of "fatiguing" begin. You need add nothing more, to know, as you eat, that life, so long as salads are left to us, is well worth the living.

To say this is to differ in a measure from the great Alexandre, a misfortune surely to be avoided. To this lettuce he would add herbs of every kind; nay, even oysters, or tortoise eggs, or anchovies, or olives—in fact, the subject is one which has sent his ever delightful imagination to work most riotously. But, in all humility, must it still be urged that the cabbage lettuce is best ungarnished, save, it may be, by a touch of the unrivalled celery or slices of the adorable tomato—never, if yours be the heart of an artist, by the smallest fragment of the coarse, crude, stupid beetroot.

The *romaine*, or *cos*, however, is none the worse for Dumas' suggestions; indeed, it is much the better. Its long stiff leaves, as they are, may not be "fatigued" with anything approaching ease or success. It is to be said—with hesitation perhaps, and yet to be said—that they make the better salad for being cut before they are put into the bowl As if to atone for this unavoidable liberty, dainty additions may not come amiss: the tender little boneless anchovies, fish of almost any and every kind—most admirably, salmon and a bit of red herring in conjunction—cucumbers, celery, tomatoes, radishes—all will blend well and harmoniously. Be bold in your experiments, and fear nothing. Many failures are a paltry price to pay for one perfect dish.

Of other green salads the name is legion: endive, dandelion leaves, chicory, chervil, mustard and cress, and a hundred and more besides before the resources of France—more especially the Midi—and Italy be exhausted. And none may be eaten becomingly without the oil and vinegar dressing; all are the pleasanter for the *soupçon* of onion, and the egg, hard-boiled; a few gain by more variegated garniture.

But these minor salads—as they might be classed—pale before the glories of the tomato: the *pomodoro* of the Italian, the *pomme d'amour* of the Provençal—sweet, musical names, that linger tenderly on the lips. And, indeed, if the tomato were veritably the "love apple" of the Scriptures, and, in Adam's proprietorship, the olives already yielded oil, the vines vinegar, then the tragedy in the Garden of Eden may be explained without the aid of commentary. Many a man—Esau notably—has sold his birthright for less than a good tomato salad.

Dante's *Inferno* were too good for the depraved who prepare it, as if it were a paltry pickle, with a dosing of vinegar. It must first receive the stimulus of the onion; then its dressing must be fortified by the least suspicion of mustard—English, French, or German, it matters not which—and if the pleasure that follows does not reconcile you to Paradise lost, as well might you live on dry bread and cold water for the rest of your natural days. The joys of the epicure, clearly, are not for you. It seems base and sordid to offer for so exquisite a delicacy hygienic references. But the world is still full of misguided men who prize "dietetic principles" above the delights of gluttony; once assured that from the eating of the tomato will come none of the evils "to which flesh is *erroneously supposed* to be heir," they might be induced to put tomato salad, made in right fashion, to the test. Then must they be confirmed faddists indeed, if they do not learn that one eats not merely to digest.

To the mystical German, the potato first revealed virtues undreamed of by the blind who had thought it but a cheap article of food to satisfy hunger, even by the French who had carried it to such sublime heights in their *purées* and *soufflés*, their *Parisiennes* and *Lyonnaises*. Not until it has been allowed to cool, been cut in thin slices, been dressed as a salad, were its subtlest charms suspected. To the German— to that outer barbarian of the mid-day dinner— we owe at least this one great debt of gratitude. Like none other, does the potato-salad lend itself to the most fantastic play of fancy. It stimulates imagination, it awakens ambition. A thousand and one ways there be of preparing it, each better than the last. With celery, with carrots, with tomatoes, with radishes, with parsley, with cucumber, with every green thing that grows—in greatest perfection with okras, the vegetable dear to Hungarian and American, unknown to poor Britons—it combines graciously and deliciously, each combination a new ecstasy. And, moreover, it is capable of endless decoration; any woman with a grain of ingenuity can make of it a thing of beauty, to look upon which is to sharpen the dullest appetite. So decorative are its possibilities, that at times it is a struggle to decide between its merits as an ornament and its qualities as a delicacy. For truth is, it becomes all the more palatable if dressed and "fatigued" an hour or so before it is eaten, and the oil and vinegar given time to soak through every slice and fragment. The wise will disdain, for the purpose, the ordinary potato, but procure instead the little, hard "salad potato," which never crumbles; it comes usually from Hamburg, and is to be bought for a trifle in the German *delicatessen* shops of London.

Poetic in the early spring is the salad of "superb asparagus"—pity it should ever be eaten hot with drawn butter!—or of artichoke, or of cucumber—the latter never fail to sprinkle with parsley, touch with onion, and "fatigue" a good half hour before serving. Later, the French bean, or the scarlet runner should be the lyrical element of the feast And in winter, when curtains are drawn and lamps lit, and fires burn bright, the substantial *Soissons*, for all its memories of French commercials, is not to be despised. But, if your soul aspires to more ethereal flights, then create a vegetable salad—cauliflower, and peas, and potatoes, and beans, and carrots in rhythmical proportions and harmonious blending of hues.

THE SALADS OF SPAIN

THEY are still many and delicious as when Beckford ate them and was glad, a hundred and more years ago. The treasures of the Incas have dwindled and disappeared; the Alhambra has decayed and been restored on its high hill-top; the masterpieces of Valasquez have been torn from palace walls, to hang in convenient rows in public museums; the greatness of Spain has long been waning. But the Spaniard still mixes his salads with the art and distinction that have been his for centuries. Herein, at least, his genius has not been dimmed, nor his success grown less. And so long as this remains true, so long will there be hope of a new Renaissance in the Iberian peninsula. By a nation's salads may you judge of its degree of civilisation; thus tested, Spain is in the van, not the rear, of all European countries.

It is no small achievement to give distinctive

character to national salads, to-day that the virtue of vinegar and oil and the infallibility of incomparable onion are universally acknowledged and respected. And yet Spain, in no idle spirit of self-puffery, can boast of this achievement. She has brought to her *insalada* a new element, not wholly unknown elsewhere —in Hungary, for instance—but one which only by the Spaniard has been fully appreciated, constantly introduced, and turned to purest profit. This element—need it be said? —is the pepper, now red, now green. The basis of the Spanish salad may be—nay, is— the same as in other lands: tomato, cucumber, lettuce, beans, potatoes. But to these is added pepper—not miserably dried and powdered, but fresh and whole, or in generous slices—and behold! a new combination is created, a new flavour evolved. And it is a flavour so strong, yet subtle withal, so aromatic and spicy, so *bizarre* and picturesque—dream-inspiring as the aroma of green Chartreuse, stimulating as Cognac of ripe years—that the wonder is its praises hitherto have not been more loudly sung, its delights more widely cultivated. The trumpet-note struck by the glowing scarlet is fitting herald of the rapturous thrills that follow in the eating. Not more voluptuous than the salad thus adorned were the beauties of the harem, who doubtless feasted upon it under the cypresses and myrtles of Andalusia.

The tendency of the Spaniard is ever to harmony, intricate and infinite. Is not his dish of dishes his *olla cocida*? Is not his favourite course of vegetables the *pisto*? And so likewise with his salads: now he may give you tomato just touched with pepper, cucumber just enlivened by the same stirring presence. But more often he will present you an arrangement which, in its elaboration, may well baffle the first investigation of the student. Peppers, as like as not of both species, tomatoes, cucumber, onion, garlic cut fine as if for a mince of greens—"pepper hash," the American crudely calls an arrangement closely akin in motive—are mingled together so deftly, are steeped in vinegar and oil so effectually, as to seem, not many in one, but *the* one in many, the crowning glory of the glorious vegetable world of the South. Nothing in common has this delectable salad with the *macédoine*, which the Spaniard also makes. Peas and carrots, potatoes and tomatoes, beans and cauliflowers meet to new purpose, when peppers, red and ardent, wander hither and thither in their midst waging war upon insipidity, destroying, as if by fire, the tame and the commonplace. Again, lettuce untainted by garlic, resisting the slightest suspicion of complexity, may answer for the foolish foreigner who knows no better. But in lettuce prepared for himself the Spaniard spares not the fragrant garlic; neither does he omit his beloved peppers, while he never rebels, rejoicing rather, if occasional slices of cucumber and tomatoes lie hid between the cool green leaves.

But fish furnishes him with text for still more eloquent flights, still loftier compositions. A *mayonnaise* he can make such as never yet was eaten under milder suns and duller skies; and a *mayonnaise* far from exhausts his all but unlimited resources. Sardines he will take, or tunny, or any fish that swims, and that, already cooked, has been either shut up long weeks in protecting tins or left but a few hours to cool.

Whatever the fish chosen, he places it neatly and confidently at the bottom of his dish; above it he lays lettuce leaves and garlic and long brilliant slices of scarlet pepper; round about it he weaves a garniture of olives and hard-boiled eggs that reveal their hearts of gold. The unrivalled, if cosmopolitan, sauce of vinegar and oil is poured upon the whole and made doubly welcome. But details are varied in every fish salad served in Spain; only in its perfection does it prove unalterable.

These, and their hundred offshoots were conceived in serious moments. But once, in sheer levity of spirit and indolence, the gay Andalusian determined to invent a salad that, to the world beyond his snowy Sierras, would seem wildest jest, but to himself would answer for food and drink, and, because of its simplicity and therefore cheapness, save him many a useless hour of gaining his dinner at the sweat of his brow. And so, to the strumming of guitars and click of castanets, now never heard save in books of travel through Andalusia, *gaspacho* appeared; destined to be for ever after the target for every travel-writer's wit, the daily fare of its inventor and his descendants. To the Andalusian *gaspacho* is as *macaroni* to the Neapolitan, *bouillabaisse* to the Provençal, chops and steaks to the Englishman. In hotels, grotesquely French or pretentiously English, where butter comes out of tins, and salad is garlicless, *gaspacho* may be but surreptitiously concocted for the secret benefit of the household. But go to the genuine Andalusian *posada* or house, travel in Andalusian boat, or breakfast at Andalusian buffet, and ten to one *gaspacho* figures on the *menu*.

To describe it, Gautier must be borrowed from. What would you? When the master has pronounced upon any given subject, why add an inefficient postscript? When a ready-made definition, admirably rendered, is at your command, why be at the pains of making a new one for yourself? Never be guilty of any work when others may do it for you, is surely the one and only golden rule of life. Listen, then, to the considerate Gautier: "*Gaspacho* deserves a description to itself, and so we shall give here the recipe which would have made the late Brillat-Savarin's hair stand on end You pour water into a soup tureen, to this water you add vinegar" (why omit the oil, you brilliant but not always reliable poet?), "shreds of garlic, onions cut in quarters, slices of cucumber, some pieces of pepper, a pinch of salt; then you add bits of bread, which are left to soak in this agreeable mess, and you serve cold." It should be further explained that, in the season, tomatoes are almost invariably introduced, that they and all the greens are chopped up very fine, and that the whole has the consistency of a *julienne* supplied with an unusually lavish quantity of vegetables. It is eaten with a spoon from a soup plate, though on the *menu* it appears as a course just before the sweets. This explanation made, listen again to Gautier, who writes in frivolous mood. "With us, dogs but tolerably well bred would refuse to compromise their noses in such a mixture. It is the favourite dish of the Andalusians, and the prettiest women, without fear, swallow at evening great spoonfuls of this infernal soup. *Gaspacho* is held to be most refreshing, an opinion which to us seems a trifle daring, and yet, extraordinary as it may be found at the first taste, you finish by accustoming yourself to it, and even liking it."

He was right. *Gaspacho* has its good points: it is pleasant to the taste, piquant in its very absurdity; it is refreshing, better than richly-spiced sauces when the sun shines hot at midday. Andalusians have not been labouring under a delusion these many years. The pepper is a stimulant; vinegar, oil, and water unite in a drink more cooling and thirst-quenching than abominable red wine of Valdepeñas. Would you be luxurious, would you have your *gaspacho* differ somewhat from the poor man's, drop in a lump of ice, and double will be your pleasure in the eating.

Like all good things *gaspacho* has received that sincerest form of flattery, imitation; and, what is more gratifying, received it at home. Lettuce, cut in tiny pieces, is set floating in a large bowl of water, vinegar, and oil, well seasoned with salt. Refreshing this also is claimed to be; though so strange a sight is it to the uninitiated that a prim schoolma'am, strayed from Miss Wilkins's stories into Andalusia, has been seen to throw up hands of wonder, and heard to declare that that salad would find a niche in her diary, to which, as a rule, she confided nothing less precious than her thoughts. Happy Spain, to have so conquered! What is Granada to the possession of so chaste a tribute?

THE STIRRING SAVOURY

First impressions have their value: they may not be dismissed in flippancy of spirit. But for this reason must last impressions be held things of nought, not worthy the consideration of ambitious or intelligent man? First impressions at times are washed away by the rich, fast stream of after-events, even as the first on a slate disappear under the obliterating sponge; last impressions remain to bear testimony after the more tangible facts have passed into the *ewigkeit*. Else, where the use of the ballade's *envoy*, of the final sweet or stirring scene as the curtain falls upon the play?

It is the same with all the arts—with love, too, for that matter, were there but space to prove it. Love, however, dwindles in importance when there is question of dinner or breakfast. Life consists of eating and drinking, as greater philosophers than Sir Andrew Aguecheek have learned to their infinite delight, have preached to the solace of others. Therefore, so order your life that the last impressions of your eating and drinking may be more joyful, more beautiful than the first; then, and only then, will you have solved that problem of problems which, since the world began, has set many a Galahad upon long and weary quest. It behoves you to see that the feast, which opened with ecstasy, does not close with platitude, and thus cover you with shame and confusion. A paltry amateur, a clumsy bungler, is he who squanders all his talent upon the soup, and leaves the savoury to take care of itself. Be warned in time!

The patriotic claim the savoury as England's invention. Their patriotism is pretty and pleasing; moreover, it is not without a glimmering of truth. For to England belongs the glorious discovery that the dinner which ends with a savoury ends with rapture that passeth human understanding! The thing itself has its near of kin, its ancestors, as one might say. Caviar, olives, lax, anchovies, herrings' roe, sardines, and as many more of the large and noble family—do not these appear as *antipasti* in Italy? In Russia and Scandinavia do they not, spread symmetrically on side table, serve the purpose of America's cocktail? And among the palms, as among the pines, coldness is held to be an essential quality in them. Hot from the ardent oven, the Parisian welcomes their presence between the soup and the fish, and many are the enthusiasts who declare this to be the one and only time for their discreet appearance upon the *menu*. Reason is in the plea: none but the narrow-minded would condemn it untested and untried. He who prizes change, who rebels even against the monotony of the perfect, may now and again follow this fashion so gaily applauded by *gourmets* of distinction. But, remembering the *much* that depends upon last impressions, the wise will reserve his savoury to make therewith a fair, brave ending.

There still walk upon this brutal earth poor heedless women who, in the innocence of their hearts, believe that the one destiny of cheese is to lie, cut up in little pieces, in a three-cornered dish, which it shares with misplaced biscuits and well-meaning rolls of butter, and, it may be, chilling celery. But cheese, which in many ways has achieved such marvels, may be wrought into savouries beyond compare. As *soufflé*, either *au Gruyère* or *au Parmesan*, it becomes light and dainty as the poet's lyric, and surely should be served only on porcelain of the finest. It is simple to say how the miracle is worked: a well-heated oven, a proper saucepan, butter, water, pepper, salt and sugar in becoming proportions, the yolks of eggs and grated Parmesan, the whites of the eggs added, as if an afterthought; and twenty-five minutes in the expectant oven will do the rest. But was ever lyric turned out by rule and measure? Even the inspired artist has been known to fail with his *soufflé*. Here, indeed, is a miracle, best entrusted to none but the genius.

Canapé au Parmesan has pretensions which the result justifies. On the bread, fried as golden as the haloes of Fra Angelico's angels, the grated Parmesan, mingled with salt and pepper, is spread. A Dutch oven yields temporary asylum until the cheese be melted, when, quicker than thought, the *canapés* are set upon a pretty dish and served to happy mortals. *Ramaquins* of cheese, in cases or out, can boast of charms the most seductive. Nor in *gougère* or *beignet* or *bouchée* will Parmesan betray confidence. Again, in *pailles*, or straws, on fire with cayenne, and tied with fluttering ribbons into enticing bunches, this happy child of the South reveals new powers of seduction. So long as there is cheese to command, the most fastidious need not wander far in search of savouries.

The anchovy may be made a dangerous rival to Parmesan. Whole, or in paste, it yields enchanting harmonies, burning and fervent as lover's prayer. Let your choice fall upon the boneless anchovies of France, if you would aim at the maximum of pleasure and the minimum of labour. True it is that labour in the kitchen is ever a joy; but, expended upon one creation when it might be divided among many, must not sacrifice of variety in sensation be the price paid? Fried after the fashion of whitebait, sprinkled with *paprika*, and refreshed with lemon juice, anchovies become quite irresistible as *Orlys d'anchois*. Prepared in cases, like Parmesan, they are proof against criticism as *tartelettes*. Now figuring as *petites bouchées*, now as *rissolettes*, they fail not to awaken new and delicious emotions. They simply clamour for certain exquisite combinations, to-day with hard-boiled egg passed through a sieve, to-morrow with olives from sunny Provence; thin brown bread and butter, or toast, the crisp foundation. But rarely do they go masquerading so riotously as in the garb of *croûtes d'anchois:* first, the golden *croûton*, then a slice of tomato, then a slice of cucumber, then a layer of caviar, then a layer of anchovies scarlet with *paprika* and garnished with leaves of chervil; and behold! you have a pyramid more memorable far than any raised on Egyptian sands— a pyramid that you need not travel silly miles to see: it is yours, any day and any hour, for the ordering.

Lax laid lightly on toast is a pale rose triumph. *Olives farcies*—caper and anchovy chief ingredients of the *farce*—come like a flaming ray of southern sunlight. Haddock is smoked in the land across the border solely that it may ravish the elect in its grandest phase as *croustades de merluche fumée*. By the shores of the blue Mediterranean, sardines are packed in tins that the delicate diner of the far north may know pleasure's crown of pleasure in *canapé de sardines diablées*. Caviar craves no more elaborate seasoning than lemon juice and *paprika* can give; herring roe sighs for devilled biscuit as friendly resting-place. Shrimp and lobster vie with one another for the honour either *bouchée* or *canapé* bestows. And ham and tongue pray eagerly to be grated and transformed into bewildering *croûtes*. The ever-willing mushroom refuses to be outsped in the blessed contest, but murmurs audibly, "*Au gratin* I am adorable;" while the egg whispers, "Stuff me, and the roses and raptures are yours!"

But what would the art of eating be without the egg? In two strange and striking combinations it carries the savoury to the topmost rung in the ladder of gastronomy. Its union with inexhaustible anchovy and Bombay duck has for issue "Bombay toast," the very name whereof has brought new hope to staid dons and earnest scholars. Pledged to anchovies once more and butter and cream—Mormon-like in its choice of many mates—it offers as result "Scotch woodcock," a challenge to fill high the glass with Claret red and rare.

Endless is the stimulating list. For cannot the humble bloater be pressed into service, and the modest cod? Do not many more vegetables than spinach, that plays so strong a part in *Raviole à la Genoese*, answer promptly when called upon for aid? And what of the gherkin? What of the almond—the almond mingled with caviar and cayenne? And what of this, that, and the other, and ingenious combinations by the score? Be enterprising! Be original! And success awaits you.

INDISPENSABLE CHEESE

With bread and cheese and kisses for daily fare, life is held to be perfect by the poet. But love may grow bitter before cheese loses its savour. Therefore the wise, who value the pleasures of the table above tender dalliance, put their faith in strong Limburger or fragrant Brie, rather than in empty kisses. If only this lesson of wisdom could be mastered by all men and women, how much less cruel life might be!

Nor is cheese without its poetry to comfort the hater of pure prose. Once the "glory of fair Sicily," there must ever linger about it sweet echoes of Sicilian song sung under the wild olives and beneath the elms, where Theocritus "watched the visionary flocks." Did not "a great white cream-cheese" buy that wondrous bowl—the "miracle of varied work"—for which Thyrsis sang the pastoral song? Cheese-fed were the shepherds who piped in the shadow of the ilex tree, while the calves were dancing in the soft green grass; cheese-scented was the breath of the fair maidens and beautiful youths they loved. Is there a woman with soul so dead, who, when in a little country inn fresh cheese is laid before her, cannot fancy that she sees the goats and kids among the tamarisks of the sun-kissed Sicilian hills, and hears the perfect voices of Daphnis and Menalcas, the two herdsmen "skilled in song"?

Perhaps because cheese has been relegated to the last course at midday breakfast, or at dinner, has it lost much of its charm for the heedless. But who, indeed, playing with peach or orange at dessert, knows the fruit's true flavour as well as he who plucks it fresh from the tree while wandering through the peach orchards of Delaware or the orange groves of Florida? Take a long walk over the moors and through the heather, or cycle for hours along winding lanes, and then, at noon, eat a lunch of bread and cheese, and—even without the kisses—you will find in the frugal fare a godlike banquet. Time was when bits cut from the huge carcase of a well-battered Cheddar, washed down with foaming shandygaff, seemed more delicious far than the choicest dishes at the Lapérouse or Voisin's. Memory journeys back with joy to the fragrant, tough, little goat's cheese, with flask of Chianti, set out upon the rough wooden table in front of some wayside vine-trellised *albergo*, while traveller and cycle rested at the hour when shade is most pleasant to men How many a tramp, through the valleys and over the passes of Switzerland, has been made the easier by the substantial slice of good Gruyère and the cup of wine well cooled in near snow-drifts! How many rides awheel through the pleasant land of France have been the swifter for the Camembert and roll devoured by the way!

Places and hours there are when cheese is best. But seldom is it wholly unwelcome. From dinner, whatever may then be its limitations, some think it must never be omitted. Remember, they say, as well a woman with but one eye as a last course without cheese. But see that you show sympathy and discretion in selecting the variety most in harmony with your *menu*, or else the epicure's labours will indeed be lost. It is not enough to visit the cheesemonger's, and to accept any and every kind offered. The matter is one requiring time and thought and long experience. You must understand the possibilities of each cheese chosen, you must bear in mind the special requirements of each meal prepared. Preposterous it would be truly to serve the mild flavoured plebeian species from Canada or America after a carefully ordered dinner at Verrey's; wasteful, to use adorable Port Salut or aromatic Rocquefort for a pudding or a Welsh rabbit.

Study gastronomic proprieties, cultivate your imagination, and as the days follow each other fewer will be your mistakes. Heavy Stilton and nutritious Cheddar, you will know, belong by right to undisguised joint and irrepressible greens. to a "good old-fashioned English dinner" they prove becoming accompaniments. Excellent they are, after their fashion, to be honoured and respected; but something of the seriousness and the stolidity of their native land has entered into them, and to gayer, more frivolous moods they are as unsuited as a sermon to a ballroom. If, however, to the joint you cling with tenacity, and solemn Stilton be the cheese of your election, do not fail to ripen it with port of the finest vintage or good old ale gently poured into holes, here and there scooped out for the purpose, and then filled once more with the cheese itself.

Strength, fierce in perfume and flavour alike, lies in Limburger, but it is strength which demands not beef or mutton, but *wurst* and *sauerkraut*. Take it not home with you, unless you would place a highly-scented barrier between yourself and your friends; but, in deep thankfulness of heart, eat it after you have lunched well and heartily in the Vienna Café, which overlooks Leicester Square, or in that other which commands Mudie's and Oxford Street. And thanks will be deepened a hundredfold if, while eating, you call for a long refreshing draught of Munich beer.

Sweet, redolent of herbs, are gracious Gorgonzola, of which such ribald tales are told by the irreverent, and royal Rocquefort, in its silver wrapping; eaten after "the perfect dinner," each has merit immeasurable—merit heightened by a glass of Beaune or Chambertin. Then, too, is the hour for Port Salut, with its soothing suggestion of monastic peace and contentment, alone a safeguard against indigestion and other unspeakable horrors; if you respect your appetite seek it nowhere save in the German *delicatessen* shop, but there order it with an easy conscience and confidence in the white-coated, white-aproned ministering spirit at the counter. Thither also turn for good Camembert; but, as you hope for pleasure in the eating, be not too ready to accept the first box offered: test the cheese within with sensitive finger, and value it according to its softness, for an unripe Camembert, that crumbles at touch of the knife, is deadlier far than all the seven deadly sins. It should be soft and flowing almost as languid *Fromage de Brie*, indolent and melting on its couch of straw. Beyond all cheese, Gruyère calls for study and reflection, so many are the shams, by an unscrupulous market furnished, in its place. As palely yellow as a Liberty scarf, as riddled with holes as cellular cotton, it should be sweet as Port Salut, and yet with a reserve of strength that makes it the rival of Limburger.

But blessed among cheeses, a romance in

itself, is the creamy, subtle little *Suisse*, delectable as Dumas calls it. Soft and sweet as the breath of spring, it belongs to the season of lilacs and love. Its name evokes a vision of Paris, radiant in the Maytime, the long avenues and boulevards all white and pink with blossoming horse-chestnuts, the air heavy laden with the fragrance of flowers; a vision of the accustomed corner in the old restaurant looking out upon the Seine, and of the paternal waiter bearing the fresh *Suisse* on dainty green leaf. Life holds few such thrilling interludes! You may eat it with salt, and think yourself old and wise; but why not be true to the spirit of spring? Why not let yourself go a little, and, eating your *Suisse* with sugar, be young and foolish and unreasonably happy again?

Authorities there be who rank the *Broccio* of Corsica above the *Suisse*, and credit it with delicious freshness and Virgilian flavour. To taste it among its wild hills, then, would be well worth the long journey to the island in the Medeiterranean. In the meantime, however, none need quarrel with *Suisse*. Hardly a country or district in the world really that has not its own special cheese; he who would discover them all and catalogue them must needs write a treatise on geography.

But to eat cheese in its many varieties, with butter or salt or sugar, as the case may be, and to think its mission thus fulfilled, would be to under-estimate its inexhaustible resources. Innumerable are the masterpieces the culinary artist will make of it. In an omelet you would pronounce it unsurpassable, so long as kind fate did not set before you the consummate *Fondue*. As a pudding you would declare it not to be approached, if sometimes crisp cheese straws were not served with dinner's last course. On an ocean voyage, Welsh-rabbit late at night will seem to you the marvel of marvels; on a railway journey a cheese sandwich at noon you will think still more miraculous—but let the sandwich be made of brown bread, and mix butter and mustard and anchovies with the cheese. The wonders that may be worked with Parmesan alone—whether in conjunction with *macaroni*, or soup, or cauliflower, or many a dish beside—would be eloquent text for a new chapter.

A STUDY IN GREEN AND RED

You may search from end to end of the vast Louvre; you may wander from room to room in England's National Gallery; you may travel to the Pitti, to the Ryks Museum, to the Prado; and no richer, more stirring arrangement of colour will you find than in that corner of your kitchen garden where June's strawberries grow ripe. From under the green of broad leaves the red fruit looks out and up to the sun in splendour unsurpassed by paint upon canvas. And the country, with lavish prodigality born of great plenty, takes pity upon the drear, drab town, and, packing this glory of colour in baskets and crates, despatches it to adorn greengrocer's window and costermonger's cart "Strawberries all ripe, sixpence a pound," is the itinerant sign which now sends a thrill through Fleet Street and brings joy to the Strand.

To modern weakling the strawberry is strong

with the strength of classical approval. The Greek loved it; the Latin vied with him in the ardour of his affection. Poets sang its wonders and immortalised its charms. Its perfume was sweet in the nostrils of Virgil; its flavour enraptured the palate of Ovid; and at banquets under the shadow of the Acropolis and on sunny Pincian Hill, the strawberry, cultivated and wild, held place of honour among the dear fruits of the earth

Nor did it disappear before the barbarian's inroads. Europe might be laid waste; beauty and learning and art might be aliens in the land that was once their home; human enjoyment might centre upon a millennium to come rather than upon delights already warm within men's grasp. But still the strawberry survived. Life grew ugly and rue and barren. But from under broad leaves the little red fruit still looked out and up to the sun; and, by loveliness of colour and form, of flavour and scent, proved one of the chief factors in reclaiming man from barbarism, in leading him gently along the high road to civilisation and the joy of life.

Respect for its exquisite perfection was ever deep and heartfelt. Gooseberries might be turned to wine and figure as fools; raspberries and currants might be imprisoned within stodgy puddings. But the strawberry, giver of health, creator of pleasure, seldom was submitted to desecration by fire. As it ripened, thus was it eaten: cool, scarlet, and adorable. At times when, according to the shifting of the seasons, its presence no longer made glad the hearts of its lovers, desire invented a substitute. As the deserted swain takes what cold comfort he can from the portrait of his mistress, so the faithful stayed themselves with the strawberry's counterfeit. And thus was it made: "Take the paste of Massepain, and roul it in your hands in form of a Strawberry, then wet it in the juice of Barberries or red Gooseberries, turn them about in this juice pretty hard, then take them out and put them into a dish and dry them before a fire, then wet them again for three or four times together in the same juice, and they will seem like perfect Strawberries." Master Cook Giles Rose is the authority, and none knew better.

If, in moment of folly, in an effort to escape monotony, however sweet, the strawberry was robbed of its freshness, it was that it might be enclosed in a tart. Then—how account for man's inconsistency?—it was so disguised, so modified by this, that, or the other companion in misery, that it seemed less a strawberry than ever Master Rose's ingenious counterfeit. And, in witness thereof, read Robert May, the Accomplished Cook, his recipe: "Wash the strawberries and put them into the tart; season them with cinnamon, ginger, and a little red wine, then put on the sugar, bake it half an hour, ice it, scrape on sugar, and serve it." A pretty mess, in truth, and yet, for sentiment's sake, worth repetition in this degenerate latter day Queen Anne preserved the tradition of her Stuart forefathers, and in "The Queen's Royal Cooker," a little book graced by the Royal portrait, Robert May's tart reappears, cinnamon, ginger, and all. So it was handed down from generation to generation, cropping up here and there with mild persistency, and now at last, after long career of unpopularity, receiving distinction anew.

One tart in a season, as tribute to the past, will suffice. It were a shame to defile the delicate fruit in more unstinted quantities. Reserve it rather for dessert, that in fragile porcelain dish or frail glass bowl it may lose nothing of the fragrance and crispness and glow of colour that distinguished it as it lay upon the brown earth under cool green shelter. To let it retain unto the very last its little green stem is to lend to dinner or breakfast table the same stirring, splendid harmony that lit up, as with a flame, the kitchen garden's memorable corner. But if with cream the fruit is to be eaten, then comfort and elegance insist upon green stem's removal before ever the bowl be filled or the dish receive its dainty burden.

At early "little breakfast" of coffee and rolls, or tea and toast, as you will, what more delicious, what fresher beginning to the day's heat and struggles, then the plate of strawberries newly picked from their bed? Banish cream and sugar from this initiative meal. At the dawn of daily duty and pleasure, food should be light and airy and unsubstantial. Then the stem, clinging fast to the fruit's luscious flesh, is surely in place. Half the delight is in plucking the berry from the plate as if from the bush.

After midday breakfast, after evening dinner, however, it is another matter. Cream now is in order; cream, thick and sweet and pure, covering the departing strawberry with a white pall, as loving and tender as the snow that protects desolate pastures and defenceless slopes from winter's icy, inexorable fingers. Sprinkle sugar with the cream, as flowers might be strewn before the altars of Dionysius and Demeter.

Cream may, for time being, seem wholly without rivals as the strawberry's mate, the two joined together by a bond that no man would dare put asunder. But the strawberry has been proven fickle in its loves—a very Cressida among fruits. For to Kirsch it offers ecstatic welcome, while Champagne meets with no less riotous greeting. To Cognac it will dispense its favours with easy graciousness, and from the hot embrace of Maraschino it makes no endeavour to escape. Now, it may seem as simple and guileless as Chloe, and again as wily and well-versed as Egypt's far-famed Queen. But with the results of its several unions who will dare find fault? In each it reveals new, unsuspecting qualities, subtle and ravishing. On pretty, white-draped teatable, rose-embowered, carnation-scented, the strawberry figures to fairest advantage when Champagne holds it in thrall; in this hour and bower cream would savour of undue heaviness, would reveal itself all too substantial and palpable a lover. Again, when elaborate dinner draws to an end, and dessert follows upon long procession of soup and fish and *entrées* and roasts and vegetables and salads and poultry and sweets and savouries, and who knows what—then the strawberry becomes most irresistible upon yielding itself, a willing victim, to the bold demands of Kirsch. A *macédoine* of Kirsch-drowned strawberries, iced to a point, is a dish for which gods might languish without shame.

She who loves justice never fears to tell the whole truth and nothing but the truth. To cook the strawberry is to rob it of its sweetest bloom and freshness. But there have been others to think otherwise, as it must in fairness be added. To the American, strawberry short-cake represents one of the summits of earthly bliss. In ices, many will see the little fruit buried without a pang of regret; and the device has its merits. As syrup, distended with soda-water and ice-cream, the conservative Londoner may now drink it at Fuller's. In the flat, open, national tart, the Frenchman places it, and congratulates himself upon the work of art which is the outcome. Or, accepting Gouffé as master, he will soar, one day, to the extraordinary heights of *coupe en nougat garnie de fraises*, and find a flamboyant colour-print to serve as guide; the next he will descend to the mere homeliness of *biegnets de fraises*; and, as he waxes more adventurous, he will produce *bouchées de dame*, or *pain à la duchesse*, *madeleines en surprise* or *profiteroles*, each and all with the strawberry for motive. The spirit of enterprise is to be commended, and not one of Gouffé's list but will repay the student in wealth of experience gained. The lover, however, finds it not always easy to remember the student within him, and if joy in the eating be his chief ambition, he will be constant to the fresh fruit ever.

A MESSAGE FROM THE SOUTH

What know we of the orange in our barbarous North? To us it is an alien, a makeshift, that answers well when, our own harvests over, winter, sterile and gloomy, settles upon the land. But in the joyous South all the year round it ripens, its golden liquid a solace when heat and dust parch the throat, as when winds from the frozen North blow with unwonted cold. The tree that bears it is as eager to produce as the mothers of Israel, and, in its haste and impatience, often it whitens its branches with blossoms while still they glow with fruit, even as Beckford long since saw them in the groves of Naples.

Bright, rich colour the costermonger's barrow, piled high with oranges from distant Southern shores, gives to London's dingy streets; and not a greengrocer's window but takes on new beauty and resplendence when decorated by the brilliant heaps. But meretricious seems the loveliness of the orange here, when once it has been seen hanging from heavy-laden boughs, gleaming between cool dark leaves in its own home, whether on Guadalquivir's banks or Naples' bay, whether in western Florida or eastern Jaffa. What has a fruit that languishes in the garden of Lindajara and basks in Amalfi's sunshine, to do with London costermongers and fog-drenched shops?

Wearied and jaded by the long journey, disheartened by the injustice done to it when plucked in its young, green immaturity, it grows sour and bitter by the way, until, when it comes to the country of its exile, but a faint, feeble suggestion of its original flavour remains. With us, for instance, does not the orange of Valencia mean a little, thin-skinned, acid, miserable fruit, only endurable when smothered in sugar or drowned in Cognac? But eaten in Valencia, what is it then and there? Large and ample are its seductive proportions; its skin, deeply, gloriously golden, forswears all meagreness, though never too thick to shut out the mellowing sunshine; its juice flows in splendid streams as if to vie with the Sierra's quenchless springs; and the fruit is soft and sweet as the sweet, soft Southern maidens whose white teeth meet and gleam in its pulp of pure, uncontaminated gold. A fruit this for romance—a fruit for the Houris of Paradise; not to be peddled about in brutal barrows among feather-bearing 'Arriets.

In the South, it were a crime not to eat this fruit, created for the immortals, just as God made it. Sugar could be added but to its dishonour; the pots and pans of the sacrilegious cook would be desecration unspeakable. Feast then, upon its natural charms, and as the hot Southern breeze brings to you the scent of strange Southern blossoms, and the sky stretches blindingly blue above, and *One* sits at your side feasting in silent sympathy, fancy yourself, if you will, the new Adam—or Eve—for whom the flaming swords have been lowered, and the long-closed gates of the Garden of Eden thrown wide open.

But in the North, banish romance, banish imagination; bring to the study of the orange the prose of necessity, and realism of the earnest student. And sometimes, from prose—who knows?—poetry may spring; from realism will be evolved wild dreaming.

If the orange be from Jaffa, or "hail" from Florida, and care bestowed upon it during its long voyaging, then will it need no Northern artifice to enhance the pleasure in its power to give. True that something—much, indeed—it will have lost; but something of its Southern, spicy, subtle sweetness still survives—of the Orient's glamour, of the mystery of the Western wilderness of flower and fruit. Eat it, therefore, as it is, unadorned, unspoiled. Tear away tenderly the covering that cleaves to it so closely; tear the fruit apart with intelligent fingers; to cut it is to sacrifice its cooling juice to inanimate china, and to deprive yourself of the first freshness of its charms.

When, however, as generally—to our sorrow, be it said—the orange arrives a parody of itself, it were better to join it to one of its several dearest affinities. In well-selected company, it may recover the shadow, and more, of the splendour it elsewhere enjoys in solitary state.

Thus disguised, it may wander from dessert to the course of sweets, and by so wandering save the resourceless from the monotony of rice and rizine, batter and bread-and-butter puddings, whose fitting realm is the nursery, and from an eternity of tarts which do not, like a good design, gain by repetition. In cocoanut, the orange recognises a fellow exile, and the two, coming together, yield a new flavour, a new delight. For this purpose, the orange must be cut that the juice may flow, and if in symmetrical rounds, the effect will be more satisfying to the critical. Let the slices be laid at once in the bowl destined to hold them at the moment of serving, that not a drop of juice may escape, and arrange them so that over every layer of orange reposes a layer of sugar. Then taking the cocoanut that has been well drained, grate it as fine as patience will allow; under it bury the orange until the gold is all concealed, and the dish looks white and light and soft as the driven snow. No harm will be done, but, on the contrary, much good, by preparing some hours before dinner. It is a pretty conceit; half unwillingly the spoon disturbs this summery snow-field. But well that it does, for the combination pleases the palate no less than the eye. The orange summons forth the most excellent qualities of the cocoanut; the cocoanut suppresses the acidity and crudeness of the expatriated orange.

With sugar alone, the orange—of this secondary order be it remembered—comes not amiss, when the soul yearns for placidness and peace. If more stirring sensations be craved, baste the cut-up oranges and sugar with Cognac, and eat to your own edification. Again prepare some hours before serving, and be not stingy with the Cognac: keep basting constantly; and be certain that if the result please you not, the fault lies not with the fruit and spirits, both exultant in the unexpected union

The conservative, unused to such devices, envelop oranges in soulless fritters and imprison them in stodgy puddings. Beware their example! One followed, there is no telling the depths of plodding imbecility to which you may be plunged. Not for the frying-pan or the pudding-bowl was the golden fruit predestined. Better eat no sweets whatever than thus degrade the orange and reveal our own shortcomings.

Who will deny that in the world's great drinks the orange has played its part with much distinction? In bitters it is supreme, if gin in due proportions be added. And where would mankind be by now, had the orange-evolved liqueurs remained undiscovered? How many happy after-dinner hours would never have been! How insipid the flavour of Claret and Champagne-cup! Even temperance drinks may be endured when orange is their basis Go to Madrid or Granada, drink *beb'da helada de naranja*, and confess that in Spain the teetotallers, if any such exist, have their compensation. A *purée neigeuse, une espèce de glace liquide*, Gautier described it in a moment of expansion; and, when art is in question, what Gautier has praised who would revile? With the Spanish *bebida de naranja*, the American orange water ice may dispute the palm.

In humbler incarnation it appears as marmalade, without which the well-regulated household can do as little as without sapolio or Reckitt's blue. Who throughout the British

Isles does not know the name of Keiller? Bread and butter might better go than this most British of British institutions, the country's stay and support in time of peace, its bulwark when war drives Tommy Atkins into action. Thus has the North turned the South to its own everyday uses, and the fruit of poets passes into the food of millions.

In fruit salad, orange should be given a leading and conspicuous rôle, the aromatic little Tangerine competing gaily and guilelessly with the ordinary orange of commerce. There is scarce another fruit that grows with which it does not assimilate, with which it does not mingle, to the infinite advantage of the ardent *gourmet*. This, none knows better than the Spaniard, slandered sorely when reported a barbarian at table. If some of his refinements we could but imitate, artists truly we might be considered. He it is who first thought to pour upon his strawberries, not thick cream, but the delicate juice of the orange freshly cut. Here is a combination beyond compare; and is there not many another that might be tested· as profitably? Orange and apricot, orange and plum, orange and peach. Experiment; for even where failure follows, will not a new sensation have been secured? The failure need never be repeated. But to each new success will be awarded life eternal.

ENCHANTING COFFEE

A PERFECTLY wise man is he who is fully expert and skilful in the true use of sensualities, as in all other duties belonging to life. In the household where wisdom rules, dinner, from savoury *hors d'œuvre* to aromatic coffee, will be without reproach—or suspicion. The foolish devote their powers to this course or that, and in one supreme but ill-advised endeavour exhaust their every resource. Invention carries them no further than the soul; even discreet imitation cannot pilot them beyond the *entrée*. With each succeeding dish their folly becomes more obvious, until it culminates in the coffee, which, instead of the divine elixir it should be, proves but a vile, degrading concoction of chicory. Here is the chief among gastronomic tests; the hostess who knows not how to prepare a cup of coffee that will bring new light to her guests' eyes, new gaiety to their talk, is not worthy to receive them; the guest, who does not know good coffee when it is set before him deserves to be cast into outer darkness and fed for evermore upon brimstone and treacle. Better far throw pearls before swine, than pour good coffee into the cups of the indifferent.

The sympathies of the gourmand are all for the mighty ones of old—for an Epicurus in Greece, a Lucullus in Rome—to whom the gods had not yet given the greatest of their gifts, coffee. Sad indeed the banquet, dreamy the evening uncheered, unblessed by fragrant Mocha or mild Mysore Poor mortals still stood without the gates of Paradise, never once foreseeing the exquisite joys to come, unconscious of the penalty they paid for living so much too soon. And while they thus dwelt in sorrowful ignorance, shepherds, leading their flocks through sweet pasture-land, paused in their happy singing to note that the little kids and lambs, and even staid goats and sheep, waxed friskier and merrier, and frolicked with all the more light-hearted abandonment after they had browsed upon a certain berry-bearing bush. Thyme and lavender, mint and marjoram, never thus got into their little legs, and sent them flying off on such jolly rambles and led them into such unseemly antics. And the shepherds, no doubt, plucked the berry and tasted it, and found it good. And one day—who knows how?—by chance, they roasted it, and the fragrance was as incense in their nostrils. And then, another time they pounded it, and, it may be by merest accident, it fell into the water boiling over the fire for their midday meal. And thus, first, coffee was made.

To Abyssinia, otherwise an unknown factor in the history of good living, belongs the credit of producing the first coffee-drinkers. All honour where honour is due. The debt of the modern to Greece and Rome is smaller far than to that remote country which not one man in ten, to whom coffee is a daily necessity, could point out upon the map.

Arabs, wandering hither and thither, came to Abyssinia as they journeyed, and there drank the good drink and rejoiced. Among them were pious Moslems, who at times nodded over prayers, and, yawning pitifully as texts were murmured by lazy lips, knew that damnation must be their doom unless sleep were banished from their heavy eyes at prayer time. And to them as to the sheep and lambs, as to the goats and kids, the wonder-working berry brought wakefulness and gaiety. And into Arabia the Happy, they carried it in triumph, and coffee was drunk not for temporal pleasure but for spiritual uses. It kept worshippers awake and alert for the greater glory of Allah, and the faithful accepted it with praise and thanksgiving.

But, again, like the flocks in Abyssinian pastures, it made them too alert, it seems. After coffee, prayer grew frolicsome, and a faction arose to call it an intoxicant, to declare the drinking of it a sin against the Koran. Schisms followed, and heresies, and evils dire and manifold. But coffee fought a good fight against its enemies and its detractors; and from Arabia it passed to Constantinople, from Turkey to England, and so on from country to country, until in the end there was not one in Europe, or in the New World (which men had not then so long discovered), but had welcomed the berry that clears the clouded brain and stimulates the jaded body.

To all men its finest secrets have not been revealed. Dishonoured by many it has been and still is. Unspeakable liquids, some thick and muddy, others thin and and pale, borrow its name with an assurance and insolence that fool the ignorant. Chicory arrogantly and unscrupulously pretends to compete with it, and the thoughtless are deceived, and go their way through life obdurate and unrepentant, deliberately blinding themselves to the truth. Others understand not the hour and the place, and order it at strange moments and for stranger functions. Americans there be who, from thick, heavy, odious cups, drink it, plentifully weakened with milk, as the one proper and fit accompaniment for dinner; a spoonful of coffee follows a spoonful of soup; another is prelude to the joint; a second cup poisons the sweet. On the other hand, be it admitted in fairness, no coffee is purer and better than that of the American who has not fallen into such mistaken courses. And he who doubts should, without delay, drop in at Fuller's in Regent Street, or the Strand, where to taste is to believe.

In the afternoon, plump German matrons and maids gather about the coffee-pot, and fancy, poor souls! that they, of all womankind, are most discriminating in their choice of time and opportunity. Gossip flows smoothly on; household matters are placidly discussed; and the one and only end of coffee remains for them, now and always, unknown and unsuspected. In their blameless innocence and guileless confidence, may they have whatever happiness belongs by right to the race of humble and unaspiring housewives.

In England the spurious is preferred to the genuine; and rare, indeed, is the house or restaurant, the hotel or lodgings, where good coffee is the portion of blundering humanity. Over the barbarous depths into which the soul-inspiriting berry has been dragged in unhappy Albion, it is kinder to draw a veil.

But in the inscrutable East, the cradle of mysticism, where no problem discourages earnest seekers after truth, coffee may yet be had in full perfection. In the West, France is not without her children of light, and in the tall glass of the *café* or the deep bowl of the *auberge* coffee sometimes is not unworthy of the name, though chicory, the base, now threatens its ruin. However, Austria, nearer to the mother-country, makes the coffee of France seem but a paltry imitation, so delicious is the beautiful brown liquid, flowing in rich perennial streams in every *café*, gilded or more modest. And yet Austria, in her turn, is eclipsed, wholly and completely, by the home of Attila and Kossuth. Drink, if only once, coffee on the banks of the Danube, while gipsies "play divinely into your ear," and life will never more seem quite so meaningless.

It is not easy to understand why the multitude continue content with a bad substitute when the thing itself, in all its strength and sweetness, may be had for the asking. A little knowledge, a trifle more experience, and good coffee may be the solace and stimulus of the honest Briton, as of the wily Turk, the wandering Arab, and the fierce Magyar.

Know then, first, that your coffee berries must be pure and unadulterated. Turn a deaf ear to the tempter who urges economy and promises additional flavour. Against chicory, protest cannot be too urgent or violent. It is poison, rank and deadly. The liver it attacks, the nerves it destroys, and the digestion it disorganises hopelessly, disastrously. To the well-trained palate it is coarse beyond redemption. The fictitious air of strength it lends to the after-dinner cup delights the ignorant and saddens the wise. But why waste too recklessly good paper and type upon so degrading a topic? Why not say once and for all that chicory is impossible and revolting, an insult to the epicure, a cruel trial to the sybarite, a crime to the artist? Renounce it before it is too late, and put your trust in the undrugged berries from Arabia or Brazil, from Java or Porto Rico. Mocha is irreproachable, though it loses nothing when blended with Java or Mysore.

As the painter mixes his colours upon his palette until the right tint springs into being, so, if in befitting humility and patience, you blend coffee with coffee, know that the day is at hand when the perfect flavour will be born of the perfect union. From venturing to reccommend one harmony above all others, the most daring would refrain, Mocha and Java might inspire hymns of praise in Paradise; and yet many *gourmets* would yearn for a keener, stronger aroma, many sigh for a subtler. As in matters of love, for yourself must you choose and decide.

Sacrilegious indeed it were if, after infinite trouble and tender care in your choice, you delivered the blend of your heart to the indifferent roasting pans, or cylinders, of any chance grocer. Roast it yourself, so that the sweet savour thereof fills your house with delicious memories of the Eastern bazaar and the Italian *piazza*. Roast it in small quantities, no more at a time than may be needed for the "little breakfast," or the after-dinner cup. And roast it fresh for each meal. Be not led astray by the indolent and heedless who prize the saving of labour above the pleasures of drink, and, without a blush of shame, would send you to a shop to buy your berries roasted. The elect listen not to the tempting of the profane. In a saucepan, with lid, may the all-important deed be done. Or else a vessel shaped for the solemn rite may be bought. But whichever be used, let your undivided attention direct the process; else the berries will be burnt. A small piece of pure, irreproachable butter in the pan or "drum" will prove a friendly ally. While still hot, place the brown berries—carefully separating those done to a turn from the over-burnt, if any such there be—in the expectant mill, and grind at once.

If much depend upon the roasting, no less is the responsibility that rests with the grinding. The working of the mill, soft and low as heard from afar, makes most musical accompaniment to dinner's later courses. It is guarantee of excellence, certificate of merit. Thus trusted to the mill, when time presses, none of the coffee's essence can escape, none of its aroma. And there is art in the grinding: ground exceeding small it may answer for boiling, but not for filtering or dripping; and so be wary. If picturesqueness of preparation have charms for you, then discard the mill and, vying with the Turks, crush the berries in a mortar with a wooden crusher. The difference in results, though counted vast by the pedant, in truth exists not save in the imagination.

And now collect your thoughts in all seriousness and reverence, for the supreme moment has come. The berries are roasted and ground: the coffee is to be made! And how? That's the problem to the Englishwoman to whom good coffee is a mystery as unfathomable as original sin or papal infallibility. How? By a process so ridiculously easy as to be laughed to scorn by the complex modern. In all art it is the same—simplicity, the fruit of knowledge and experience, is a virtue beyond compare. But poor blind humans, groping after would-be ideals, seek the complicated, mistaking it to be the artistic. Arguing then, from their own foolish standpoint, they invent strange and weird machines in which they hope to manufacture perfection; coffee-pots, globular in shape, which must be turned suddenly, swiftly, surely, at the critical instant, else will love's labour all be lost; coffee-pots, with glass tubes up which the brown liquid rushes, then falls again, a Niagara in miniature; coffee-pots with accommodating whistles blowing shrill warning to the slothful; coffee-pots that explode, bomb-like, at the slightest provocation; coffee-pots that splutter, overflow, burst, get out of order, and, in a word, do everything that is dreadful and unseemly. Of these, one and all, fight shy. Coffee calls not for a practical engineer to run the machine.

In three ways, so simple a child may understand, so perfect a god might marvel, can the delectable drink, that gives wakefulness and a clear brain, be made. In the first place, in ordinary pot, it may be boiled, allowing a tablespoonful of the ground berries to a cup of water, taking the pot off the fire, once the beautiful, seductive brown froth is formed on the top, pouring in a small teaspoonful of water that the grounds may settle; serve without delay, linger over it lovingly, and then go forth gaily to conquer and rejoice.

In the second place—more to be commended—use a *cafétière*, or filter of tin or earthenware, the latter by preference. Place the coffee, ground not too fine, and in the same proportions, in the upper compartment Pour in slowly water that is just at the boiling point, a little only at a time, keeping the kettle always on the fire that the all-important boiling point may not be lost. and let the water filter or drip slowly through the grounds spread in a neat layer. Some there be who stand the pot or lower compartment in a pan of boiling water, and they have reason with them. Others who, when all the water has passed through to the pot below, set it to filtering, or dripping, a second time, and they are not wholly wrong. But of all things, be careful that the coffee does not cool in the process Of life's many abominations, lukewarm coffee is the most abominable.

The third of the three ways yields Turkish coffee. The special pots for the purpose, with their open tops and long handles, are to be found in one or more large Regent-street and Oxford-street shops. Get the proper vessel, since it answers best, and is, however, a pleasure to the eye, a stimulus to the imagination of all who at one happy period of their lives have dwelt in Turkey or neighbouring lands. Now, grind your coffee finer, but be faithful to the same proportions. Into the water drop first the sugar, measuring it according to your taste or mood, or leaving it out altogether if its sweetness offend you Put your pot on the fire, and when the water is boiling merrily, drop in the coffee. To a boil, as kitchen slang has it, let it come, but gay bubbles on its surface must be signal to lift off the pot; put it on the fire again, almost at once, remove it bubbling a second time, put it on again, and again remove it. This device repeated thrice will be enough, though a fourth repetition can do no harm A teaspoonful of cold water will compel unruly grounds to settle. Pour the thick, rich, brown liquid, as it breaks into beautiful yellow froth on the top, into the daintiest cups your cupboard holds, and drink it and happiness together

To add cream or milk to Turkish coffee would be a crime; nor must more sugar be dropped into its fragrant, luscious depths. Ordinary after-dinner coffee should also be drunk without cream or milk, if pleasure be the drinker's end. Indeed, a question it is whether it be ever wise to dilute or thicken coffee and tea with milk, however well boiled, with cream, however fresh. The flavour is destroyed, the aroma weakened. But black coffee with breakfast would mean to begin the day at too high a state of pressure, in undue exhilaration of spirits. To speak honestly, coffee is no less a mistake in the morning hours than Whisky-and-soda or Absinthe. But custom has sanctioned it; it has become a bad habit from one end of the Continent to the other, in innumerable otherwise wholly decorous British households But slaves of habit should wear their chains so that there is as little friction and chafing as possible. Therefore, make your morning coffee strong and aromatic and pure as if destined for after-dinner delights: but pour into it much milk; half and half would prove proportions within reason Not out of the way is it to borrow a hint from provincial France and serve *café-au-lait* in great bowls, thus tacitly placing it forever on a plane apart from *café noir*. Or else, borrow wisdom from wily Magyar and frivolous Austrian, and exquisite, dainty, decorative whipped cream heap up high on the surface of the morning cup. Take train to-morrow for Budapest; haunt its *cafés* and kiosques, from the stately Reuter to the Danube-commanding Hungaria; study their methods with diligence and sincerity; and then, if there be a spark of benevolence within you, return to preach the glad gospel of good coffee to the heathen at home. A hero you would be, worthy countryman of Nelson and of Wellington; and thus surely should you win for yourself fame, and a niche in Westminster Abbey.

CPSIA information can be obtained at www.ICGtesting.com
Printed in the USA
BVOW061234201111
276509BV00004B/31/P